The Bipolar Black Girl

Andrea Elizabeth Paul

B.O.S.S.
Publishing

Atlanta, GA

The Bipolar Black Girl

For information, contact,
B.O.S.S. Publishing
4820 Walden Lake Point
Decatur, GA 30035
sales@boss-emag.com

I have tried to recreate events, locales and conversations from my memories of them. In order to maintain their anonymity in some instances I have changed the names of individuals and places, I may have changed some identifying characteristics and details such as physical properties, occupations and places of residence.

This book is not intended as a substitute for the medical advice of physicians. The reader should regularly consult a physician in matters relating to his/her mental health and particularly with respect to any symptoms that may require diagnosis or medical attention.

Manufactured in the United States of America

ISBN 978-0-9863559-8-1

10 9 8 7 6 5 4 3 2 1

Dedication

Thank you to everyone who has dealt with me since I had been diagnosed with a mental health disorder. Thank you for understanding that my late nights, emotional outbursts, indifference, wild behavior, discouraging thoughts, and overall confusion while I try to navigate this world is a part of me and doesn't affect the way I appreciate you for being there for me when I need it the most.

Thank you to my friends and family members who do nothing but celebrate and support me with all that I do.

Special shout out to my Abilify (aripiprazole) for providing me with the late night encouragement and imagination to write this book! :-)

And a very special thank you to you for picking up this book. By doing so, you are one step closer to starting the conversation about mental illness in the black community. You understand that the stigma surrounding mental health is so rampant that you have decided to open a dialogue about it by opening this book. I thank you so much for taking that step. Next, I hope you learn what you can about mental health and become an advocate for those who cannot advocate for themselves.

Thank you, again, to all of you for being an important part of my life and my story. I hope you enjoy!

Sincerely,
Andrea E. Paul
The Bipolar Black Girl

Introduction

My heart was beating so hard and I didn't understand why. It took everything I had to continue laying in my bed and not call 911. I was scared I was having a heart attack but I knew that wasn't it.

The beating got louder and faster. At this point, I was psyching myself out. I just laid there, listening to my heart beat off rhythm. The darkness of my room engrossed me. The outward silence was deafening. And yet, my heartbeat was comforting. It was early morning and I was wide awake. The sun hadn't yet made its appearance in the sky, but my neighbors were already fidgeting with keys and car doors in the chilly breeze of the morning. Forcing myself to listen to them beginning their journeys to their respective destinations, I tried to drown out the thumping of my heart ringing in my ears.

"Come on, Jeffery! We have to go!" My older next door neighbor, Linda, called for her teenaged son, completely ignoring the fact that some people within earshot were still deep in slumber. "JEFFERY!" She yelled again for him

Introduction

to come outside so they could be on their way. I broke my gaze with the ceiling fan above my head and looked over to my phone lying next to me.

"I wonder what time it is," my mind inquired.

I couldn't ignore the sounds in my chest. My heart began to slow down, but it was so loud, it just about muted Linda scolding Jeffery when he finally came out of the house and sat in the car. I returned to my position flat on my back on my bed and commenced staring at the ceiling fan once more. It was soothing, yet bothersome to lay there. I had to do something for the anxiety building within me. If I didn't take control of it now, the rest of my day will be hell and I would be unable to function.

I took a deep breath like my psychologist taught me – filling my belly with air as I slowly inhaled through my nose and exhaled deflating my stomach. I sighed. The grey comforter covering me found its way off of my body and I sat up on the edge on my bed. "I guess my day has officially started," I said out loud speaking to no one. Going through my mind there was nothing, then there was everything. That's the thing with bipolar disorder – at least my bipolar disorder – my thoughts come and go as they

Introduction

please and there is no warning.

I took my first dose of Abilify, an antipsychotic, last night and it put me right to sleep. I'm not sure how I feel about my diagnosis changing from "basic" anxiety and depression, to bipolar disorder I. It's hard to admit, but something I have accepted... I'm crazy.

I understand some of the science and psychology behind it and a few other mental illnesses, only because I used to be a psychology major and I thought the mind was so fascinating. Why did I stray away from that? I still think psychology is amazing, but now, I have become the subject of study. It was MY mind that was now up for my own scrutiny and understanding.

I should have listened to her. She was the first to say I was manic. She is a DOCTOR... A newly minted doctor, but a DOCTOR, none the less, my thoughts started. *If I had told my psychologist about this early on, I probably wouldn't be here today.* I just knew that today was going to be a "down" day for me. I mean, after all, I was sitting on my bed thinking about what I could have done to stop my diagnosis; to yield it in its tracks. *My best friend of 20*

Introduction

years knew me. She knew me so well, she recognized when I wasn't being myself, even when I thought I was acting normal. She knew something wasn't right with me. Even though I pretended to be okay and fooled myself, I didn't fool her.

The sun began to peak over the houses in my subdivision and filled my room with a soft glow. I finally stood up thinking an hour had passed since I first opened my eyes this morning. I bent over to stretch my back and rose with no motivation to do anything more. I sat back down and looked at my reflection in the vanity mirror.

"Why didn't I listen to her?!" I scolded myself. *Maybe it was the stigma? Maybe it was the fact that she was new at her job? Maybe because "manic" sounds bad? I don't know.* I dropped my face into my hands and took another deep breath. "I'm crazy," I claimed as I shook my head in disbelief and disgust.

I picked up my iPhone and logged on to Facebook. I clicked the status button and typed. *'Here I am, a bipolar black girl. Let the adventure begin... Again. #AdventuresWithDrea.'*

Introduction

Introduction

Chapter 1

"Jeffery, let's go!" Linda, my neighbor yelled angrily from her car at her zombie-like son as he slowly walked from the house. I turned over in my bed and looked at my phone, it was 6:15am. Thanks to Linda and Jeffery, I no longer needed the alarm I set for myself, so I turned off the app that was supposed to wake me in an hour.

I sighed and stretched under the comforter and turned to look out of the window. I watched as Jeffery finally made it to the car and his mother said something to him as he sat down in the passenger seat. Jeffery slammed the door to their silver Honda Civic as Linda stepped on the gas and pulled off. They were new to the neighborhood. so I wasn't used to be awakened by such noise.

I saw as Mr. Keith across the street shut his front door and jingled his keys as he made his way to his Audi coupe. Mr. Keith was a tall, balding man who I assumed was a teacher or professor from the type of briefcase he carried. He had to be in his fifties with his younger looking face full of grey facial hair. He got into his car and drove off. The only reason I knew him was because one day, the mailman put one of his letters in my mailbox. Being a good neighbor, I hand delivered it, peaking at the name to make sure I gave it to the right person. When he opened the door, I smiled and said, "Good afternoon, are you Mr. Keith?"

He returned the smile and nodded. "Yes, I am."

"The mailman left this in my mailbox and I think it belongs to you." I handed over the plain white envelope and received his thank you as I bounced away. "You're welcome," I shouted from the sidewalk and waved as I walked back across the road. That was my last interaction with Mr. Keith, but I would watch him from my window when he would return at the end of his day. Briefcase, and what I assumed to be coffee in hand, he would check his mailbox and walk into his home just as quietly as he would leave in the morning.

I took a deep breath and rolled over to look at my ceiling fan. "Why me?" I wanted to know again. I had asked myself this question for the past three days, but this time, there was no overwhelming response of "why not me?" I justified that the reason I was given this diagnosis by the universe was to share my story and to get society to understand that black girls have mental illnesses, too. I have a message to share and I found my purpose, but today was different. I sat up in bed and thought, *I have a pretty good support system, but how did I end up here?*

<u>Bipolar.</u>

Like, not "Oh, I'm indecisive so I'll use "bipolar" as a slang term," but, like, "I really am BIPOLAR." There was no coming back. This morning, my thoughts were on a roll and I couldn't stop them. I just sat in the bed with my legs crossed listening to the sounds outside and the words churning in my brain. The psychiatrist's words kept coming to the forefront: "from this moment and forevermore, you are and will always be *bipolar.*" It just feels so… bad. So negative. So derogatory. So… dirty.

I closed my eyes and shook my head. I had accepted it. No matter how hard I try, even if I do get "fixed," I will always be *this.* Now, I understand why mental disorders are so stigmatized. It just feels that way when you wake up one morning and you *have it.* There is no coming back. I stretched my arms over my head and took another deep breath as I leaned back onto my pillow. I went through everything I had done these past 6 months to try and pinpoint what I had done wrong. Seriously. I was "committed" into a psychiatric unit. *THEY* thought I was legit crazy. If *THEY* thought so, it must be true, right? *THEY* are the professionals... I opened my eyes. Reliving the experience was too painful for me, yet it was my truth, my reality, my existence; I couldn't hide from it. I looked into the mirror on my vanity and thought about my time on the 13th floor.

I was put in a room full of people talking to themselves... well, they were talking to people they felt were right in front of them. I was in a room of people telling me things straight out of a scary movie that they believed to be true. I was in a room with people who needed to be sedated because their capacity to harm themselves or others was too much of a risk. I was legit in a room full of crazy people... But that observation was from the outside looking in. I was the only one not asleep, not talking to myself, and seemingly ready to go home. At that moment, I was the crazy one; the one who didn't belong...

Or so I thought.

They put me there for a reason. I'm mentally ill. That's why me. I am one of those crazy people on the 13th floor, too.

I took yet another meditative breath and looked at my cat who was still asleep at my feet. I just wanted to kick him for no reason. He was peacefully sleeping and I wanted to disrupt and hurt him. *Oh, god... Today is not going to be a good day at all.* I have to see my psychiatrist today to tell her I won't be seeing her any longer because I'm moving. Moving from safety and security to uncertainty.

It was all on a whim. I decided to move in with one of my best friends in Cincinnati because I was ready for a change, but couldn't yet afford to venture out on my own. I woke up one day and just decided to move. There was no plan, no discussion, only statements made in passing about how fun it would be if we lived together. Our productivity skyrockets when we are together, so I can't see it being a problem. Once I came to the conclusion that I was leaving home, I began looking into psychiatric services and advocacy groups in the area. I came across NAMI, the National Alliance on Mental Illness. I have to do more research, but so far so good.

Annoyed at my thoughts, instead of kicking my fluffy, grey, mixed breed cat, I leaned over and picked him up. I was beginning to feel anxious and he could tell. He wanted no parts of me and as quickly as I picked him up, he jumped out of my hands and ran for his safe haven underneath the bed. Feeling defeated by a feline, I rolled over onto my belly and exhaled loudly. *What am I supposed to do? Am I doing the right things? What if it's all in my head...?*

*Drea, it **is** all in your head. That's the issue.*

I quickly jumped out of bed and headed towards the bathroom. I needed to shower to get my thoughts to stabilize and to just wash away my distress. I turned on the water and closed the bathroom door. As the steam fogged up the oversized mirror, I just stood there looking at myself ready to nitpick at my flaws, as per usual. I turned away and began undressing. I opened the shower curtain and stepped into the bathtub. The day was off to a bad start and I didn't know how to change it for the better. The hot water rolled off my skin and instantly relaxed me. I took a deep breath and closed my eyes. *Today will be a good day. Today will be a good day.*

I washed my body and looked for my razor so I could shave my legs. I had never really been a cutter, but figured today would be the day since I was feeling so bad. Unfortunately (fortunately, if that's how you think), there were no sharp objects in sight. I knew it was stupid and that I wouldn't actually do it, but I just wanted to feel as though I was in control. Lately, I've been feeling so out of control, it didn't make sense to me. I needed something to feel, something that put me on top of the situation. I was tired of letting my thoughts and emotions get the best of me. I let out a low sigh. *Have I really come to this low point? This isn't me. I can't handle this.* I finished bathing and stepped out the tub. I could barely recognize myself in the foggy mirror. There was nothing left for me to tell myself... nothing left for me to do at that moment, except to put my clothes on and leave.

9:28am the clock on the wall read. My appointment was for 9:30 and according to my mind, I was late. I watched as the second hand twitched its way back to the 12 and around again. The remaining 2 minutes finally passed and I was starting to panic. *What if they forgot about me? Today was the right day, right? I had the right time...* I sat in the waiting room with a bit more anxiety than earlier. Bouncing my leg, I tried to talk myself out of it. *If it was the wrong day or time, the girl at the front window would have said something. Maybe the doctor's clock is slow or she's inside with another patient. That's what you need – patience. Calm down. It's barely 9:30. Someone is coming for you.* This wasn't the first time she was late coming to get me from the waiting room; it was actually more of a routine than not. I looked at my phone in an attempt to verify the time. Yup, 9:31. She was late. *There must be another patient in there. There's no rea-…*

"Andrea?" My psychiatrist's soothing voice knocked me out of the defeatist monologue I was having in my head. I smiled at her in relief and stood up. As we walked back to the office, I took a deep breath. My mind was spinning. She closed the door behind me and asked, "what brings you in today?" Her voice was just as calming as it was the first day I met her 6 months ago.

"They told me I'm bipolar," I blurted out. I held my breath and I waited for her response. I was unsure on if there was a note in my file from my psychologist about what happened 2 weeks ago. *Did she already know? She had to, right?* I still hadn't exhaled. I just stared at her for confirmation. When she didn't say anything, I knew she wanted me to keep talking, so I let out the carbon dioxide I was holding in my chest. "Dr. Bennington had me sent to Grady because she feared for my safety. Oh, and I met all of your colleagues. Everyone there knew who you were whenever I had to tell them who my psychiatrist was."

"Oh, really? Why did she send you? How long were you there for?"

"24 hours… I just told her about how I was feeling and what I was thinking the week before. I guess she thought I would act on those feelings although I told her I was fine," I shrugged it off as though people always sent me to psych. There was no response. Dr. Williams was good for that. I knew she still wanted me to carry the conversation. "I emailed you to let you know how I was feeling that day, but you responded that you were booked up and to contact the front office to set an appointment… So here I am!" I finally smiled again, clearly, I was enthused by my own sarcasm. "What does it mean to be bipolar? What should I look out for now that I have this new diagnosis of being hypermanic?"

She paused. "Well, with bipolar disorder, mania can have you irritable, speaking faster than your brain can keep up with, risk taking behaviors, you'll have loads of energy, or you may think everything is so amazing you try to convince everyone as such. Basically, a high. You're so high up, you want others there with you or it frustrates you so bad that it's annoying."

I knew it. If all she was telling me was true, I was experiencing mania right now. I actually started feeling really good after I overcame that sense of anxiety in the waiting room. It was almost like she had saved me.

"Have you always experienced these episodes?" Dr. Williams asked looking concerned.

"I guess so," I admitted. "I always have bouts of irritability and high energy. Sometimes I hate hearing my name called... It drives me crazy."

"Mmhmm..."

"But, I came to tell you that I was moving and that I wanted to know if there was anything specific I needed to know while I'm looking for a new physician. Any resources I should look into until then?"

Dr. Williams tilted her head. "Mainly, you should watch for increased levels of irritability. It's one thing to be annoyed, but it's another to want to start a fight or have dangerous road rage."

I just looked at her. I'm from Jersey; I ALWAYS have road rage. What else could she tell me?

"Also, look for instances of risky behavior. Having multiple sexual partners and unprotected intercourse, increased drinking or drug use, and spending lots of money at once. Those are the big ones. Just do some research and try to connect your behaviors and thoughts to what you find."

Didn't she know, I already spent hours with Dr. Google?? I need new info.

"Maybe look into – where are you moving to?" She asked.

"Cincinnati."

"Why Cincinnati?"

"For school. I actually applied to the University of Cincinnati's Mental Health Counseling Master's program. It doesn't start 'til the fall, but I wanted to get a head start on life before school began." My mind began to race. *Uh-oh… Was the decision to move made in haste? Could that be considered a "risk taking behavior"? Was I manic when I decided to move? Oh well. The decision has been made and I am moving. Period.*

"That's awesome," Dr. Williams said with

a smile. "Look into the Cincinnati chapter of NAMI – N.A.M.I. – and research what services they have on Cincinnati's campus," she suggested.

"UC has a teaching hospital, so I'm sure there will be a lot of opportunities to find what I need there," I claimed as though I already knew where these services were and if they even had any.

After exchanging logistics and salutations, I left her office feeling like this visit was a waste of time. She didn't tell me anything I didn't already know and that bothered me. I took a deep breath and exhaled loudly as I pressed the elevator's down button. I couldn't wait to get back home so I could lay in the bed. I pulled out my phone and checked the time: 9:47. I had the entire day in front of me and all I wanted to do was sleep.

As I walked to my car, Facebook was calling my name. I opened the app on my iPhone and posted a status update: *'When they tell you you're crazy and you believe them…'*

Chapter 2

Why am I wide awake? It was 4:15 in the morning and I hadn't been to sleep all day, yet, here I was, ready to party like it was 1999. Sleep had not been my friend lately and I couldn't pinpoint the reason. I was just being a night owl. Despite taking my Abilify at 8:30 every night, I couldn't close my eyes.

"Do you want pinot or more moscato?" My best friend, Shannon asked me as we sat in her kitchen after downing a bottle of Sutter Home moscato wine between the 2 of us. We were up talking about why I didn't have a boyfriend and the current status of her relationship. Her and her boo were so cute together, but they had their moments. It was easy to see how much they cared for each other, but that they let their mutual bullish ways get the better of them sometimes. It was quite the roller coaster ride when it came to the two of them; even from the outside looking in.

"Might as well stick to what we know. And this moscato just tastes so good," I said, requesting more of the white wine. I was drunk.

"Moscato it is!" She opened her wine cooler and pulled out another bottle.

"You know you're getting old when you own a wine cooler," I laughed at her grandiose presentation of the wine. While I could barely keep my eyes open from my intoxication, I still didn't feel the need to lay down. Our conversation was going so well. I hadn't seen Shannon in a while, so we had a lot of catching up to do. Bright side? I wasn't drinking alone at home, in my room. I had someone to enjoy it with. After about another 15 minutes of chatting, laughing, and drinking, she called it a night. With her demanding job as a personal trainer, she had to be up in 3 hours to work with a client. She needed her rest and I couldn't stop her from being responsible. I was disappointed, but I knew it was for the better.

The door to the guest room closed gently and I crawled into the plush queen sized bed. I'm grateful she could host me while I was in town because no one had time to book a hotel all the way across town. I hated asking people for favors. It made me feel like a bother, especially to be in someone else's space. It was hard for me.

Laying there, I questioned if I was being manic or if I was just excited to see my friend after so long. *How will I be able to tell the difference?* If I feel "normal" either way, I'm going to need someone else to tell me if I'm being "extra." I can't stand being extra... Extra loud, extra random, extra obnoxious. I don't like it when others behave that way so it was only right for me to hate it when I did it.

"I love you!" Shannon's words of affirmation towards me broke the night's silence and my train of thought.

"I love you, too!" I shouted back so she could hear me across the house. I smiled and took several deep breaths and closed my eyes. Immediately, I felt dizzy. *Is it the wine? My medication mixed with the wine? Or is it just me?* I opened my eyes to make the spinning stop, but they instantly closed again. *Sleep! Oh, how I've missed you.* I didn't want to admit it, but I was finally tired. I reached for my phone and opened Snapchat. I took a picture of the dark and captioned it *'#TeamMania'* before broadcasting it to my followers. I shut my phone off and put it back in its spot next to me on the bed. With that, I was sound asleep...

For all of 2 hours.

6 am found me wide awake again. This time, soaked in sweat from thigh to toe. It literally felt

as though someone poured water on me while I was asleep. I hadn't been dreaming. *Maybe it was the medication and the wine?* I wasn't hot. In fact, I was freezing cold. *Am I sick? Why does this keep happening?* For the past month, I have been suffering from night sweats. It was very uncomfortable and I had no explanation for it. I returned my attention to my phone and made an instant appointment with Dr. Google. *'Abilify and legs sweating at night'* I typed into the search bar. I clicked on the first result from Drugs.com's forum. Someone had the same side effects I thought I had, so at least I knew it wasn't just me.

"Insomnia, night sweats, and tremors..."

I continued to read the responses on the post to get further information and confirmation on these reactions.

"Restlessness, fatigue, brain fog..."

It all began to make sense. I accepted it as my new reality and simply switched positions on the bed to avoid my wet spot. All of this <u>had</u> to be a part of my new "normal", no? Everyone wanted to pull their hair out and not sleep on this medicine. After graciously acknowledging the research I had done, I closed my eyes and fought to fall back to sleep. I heard Shannon's

4-foot-11 frame walking past my room and into the bathroom. She was preparing to start her day and I was still trying to finish mine.

As I got dressed to travel to see my other best friends in Columbus, I knew something wasn't right. *I should just reschedule. I'll be here all week.* I was having an overwhelming sense of energy mixed with annoyance. I didn't want to be bothered today. *I can't today.* Even with how hyper I was feeling, I was tired. I couldn't wrap my mind around it, I just wanted to lay back down and not talk to anyone; just sleep. But I couldn't do that. I had to go see everyone, now. No one else had the freedom I did when it came to rescheduling. With Mia and Janay being hard working moms with significant others, it would be difficult to get everyone in the same space again for a while. "I can do this. It won't be hard at all," I convinced myself to not get back under the covers.

I made my way to the car and started it. "Adventure time." I put my little blue Nissan in drive and rode out of Shannon's driveway. I wish she could come with me, but you see, the way her schedule is set up, she always has to be at work. It's alright though, I still get to spend some quality time with people I love. She would join us once she was available. As I turn onto the main road, I plug the AUX cord into my phone and turn on my Pandora *NSYNC station. Whenever I take a road trip, it is absolutely necessary to blast 90s and early 2000s pop on high volume. It's the only way to stay alert during long drives.

Speeding up I-75 and singing Britney Spears' "Oops I Did It Again" as loud as humanly possible, I was basking in my nostalgia while being nervous to see my friends again after so long. *Will they think I'm crazy? Will they notice I've changed because of the medication? Will they treat me differently?* I couldn't help but to turn the volume down in the car and stop my karaoke session. *What if I still have an attitude when I get there?* I was afraid that although I was happy and excited, I felt bothered. There was no logical reason for it, I just *was*.

"In 2 miles, take the exit on the right." The GPS on my phone interrupted my worrisome thoughts. The 2 hour drive felt like 30 minutes worth of anxiety producing thoughts and I was prepared for them to spiral out of control.

Why did I even come? I questioned myself over the gentle harmony of the boyband, 98 Degrees. "Because I love them and miss them." There was no doubt that I felt a deep remorse for staying away for so long. At that moment, Captain Anxiety took off and brought his friends General Depression and Private Irrational for the ride.

"They don't miss me as much as I miss them. If they did, they would have come to see me while I was away. Hell, they would have called more."

"But the kids! I haven't seen all the babies since and a lot has happened and they are growing too fast for me not to see them. They can't travel that far to see me."

"I have to come to Columbus all the time when I move because I'll only be 2 hours away. There's no excuse to be estranged from everyone."

This internal conversation continued until I realized I reached my destination – Janay's house. I inhaled slowly and deeply. I held my breath and closed my eyes. *Everything will be great. Today will be a great day,* I thought. I exhaled sharply and opened my eyes. "Adventure time."

I parked the car on the street and got out. I looked at Janay's front door as if I wasn't jumping for joy in my heart. I felt bad because I felt bad, but I couldn't show that right now. *I'm getting to see my girls, my family, and I should be elated. I mean, I am, but I'm not.* I walked up to the door and knocked.

"Drea's here," I heard Janay say on the other side of the door before her eldest son opened it for me as if he were my host for the day.

"Hi!" I screeched, finally feeling and showing my excitement right down to my toes. I reached for him and he gave me the tightest hug he could muster for a 3 year old. "You remember me?" I asked, ready for him to look at me confused.

"You're Auntie Drea," he claimed proudly and ran towards his mother. I smiled.

"Drea!" Janay greeted me with her own tight hug and a kiss on my cheek. I really missed her and was ready to catch up and spend time with her.

"Heyyyy!" I exclaimed enthusiastically as I returned her hug.

"Mia is on her way," she said while closing the door behind me. "How was the drive?"

I took off my black North Face fleece and sat on the couch. Janay's youngest son just stared at me. "Hi!" I said, trying to not scare him with my excitement. I held my arms out in the same way I did with the oldest, but the little one did not move from his spot on the couch. I had read somewhere to not force children to hug, or even communicate with adults if they don't want to. It supposedly helps them build trust on their own terms. Plus, I knew he was a bit shy compared to his brother, so I turned my attention back to my hostess.

"The drive went by so quick. I know I'll be taking this trip all the time when I move. I have to see you guys like every week!"

Janay beamed with happiness. "Yes! Ever-ry week," she stressed.

Mia, Janay, and I were roommates and became best friends in college. To this point, we had known each other for almost 10 years. Even though they knew each other prior to meeting me, I felt like I clicked with them. I immediately felt safe and welcomed into their group. It was only a matter of time before Shannon came into the picture as our 4th member. Being a year under us, Shannon was instantly dubbed our little sister. She completed our circle.

I laughed. "Shannon just texted me. She's on her way now, too." I put my phone down and gave Janay my attention. "So, what's new? What's going on? How's married life treating you?" I asked, sincerely curious to the happenings of her life since I last saw her. I hadn't been around since her wedding, so I know something new had to have happened since then.

"Nothing's really new. Still working hard to save up to buy a house. The usual. But, we are moving next month into a bigger place. *That's* something I'm not looking forward to," she giggled.

"That's new!" I claimed, insisting that she hadn't told me about the move during our latest Glide updates.

"Yeah. You wanna help me pack?!" She joked seriously.

"I barely want to help myself pack."

"I'll pay you in wine…"

I laughed the loudest I had laughed in about 3 months. She knew my weakness and was trying to use it against me – jokingly, of course. "In that case, yes! I am so there!" We laughed and her phone buzzed. It was Mia calling to ask if she should bring anything with her.

"Tell her to hurry and bring herself. I don't

need anything," I smiled.

"Mia, Drea said, 'hurry up and bring yourself. She doesn't need anything else,'" Janay relayed the message through the phone. I sat anxiously awaiting a funny response that didn't come.

"Uh huh. Yeah… Okay. We'll see you soon. Buh-bye," was all I heard of the rest of the one sided conversation. "Are you hungry? Thirsty?"

"I'm not hungry, but I could definitely go for a glass of wine." It was early afternoon and I was ready to be a lush; even with children around. It was my vaykay and I wanted to enjoy my time with my girls. With that, Janay vanished into the kitchen.

"It's Spider Man," the little one finally said to me as he thrust his action figure into my face.

"Oh! I like Spider Man. Can I have it?" I said to him in my most early-childhood-educator voice, glad he acknowledged me on his own. He smiled and dropped the toy into my lap. I entertained him while his mother was gone; learning everything that Spider Man could do from a 2 year old with a limited vocabulary.

When Janay returned with my glass of pink moscato, I begin to worry about what she thought about my wanting to drink in the middle of the day. *Did she think I was an alcoholic or something? Do I have a problem? Why am I drinking so early?* I took a sip from the glass, trying to not let my thoughts show themselves outwardly. Thank God there was a knock on the door.

"I got it!" The voice came from upstairs and was one I was all too familiar with.

"Anisa!" I shouted. Anisa was Janay's first born daughter who we held hostage when we were at school living in the dorm. She was my little princess. Sad thing is, she wasn't little anymore. She's 8 years old now and almost as tall as me. She bounced down the steps and opened the door.

"Hi, Auntie Mia."

"Hi, Anisa," Mia exclaimed with a hug and a smile. Once they left their embrace, Anisa closed the door and headed towards me. "Hey, Auntie Drea," she said giving me a hug, also. "Where have you been?" She questioned me sarcastically.

"I've been working," I lied. "I've been really busy with school and trying to find a way to come see you!" I lied again, this time giving her a second hug. I *had* to lie. How can I tell an 8 year old that I was so mentally sick I could barely leave my bed some days? Or that I was put in a mental unit because my doctor thought I was a danger to myself. Or even that my time was consumed with psychologist and psychiatrist visits. It was hard, but I had to.

"I'm here now," I assured her. "So, how are you? How have you been?"

I forgot Spider Man was still in my lap, so when one of the boys reached for it, he snapped me out of my trance with Anisa.

"I wasn't finished playing with it, but you can have it for now," I told him. He nodded to let me know he understood.

"Everything's good," Anisa told me without much more conversation.

I reached for her hand and told her I missed her. She returned my sentiment and bounced back upstairs. She was an only child for so long before her brothers came along, she learned to keep to herself and keep herself entertained. She was the only girl, so she had to do so. The boys weren't interested in playing with her dolls or writing short stories.

"Drea, I missed you," Mia reached for me from her place on the couch next to me.

"I missed you more!" I said, hugging her as tight as I could.

Janay brought Mia a glass of water from the kitchen as she didn't want to drink wine so early in the day. That was hard for me to let go of because it was a statement that stressed me out. *Either I drink this whole glass to try and calm down or I don't drink it at all, and risk looking bothered.* I didn't drink anymore. I couldn't handle looking bad in front of my friends. 2 hours later, Shannon made her way into the house. We were complete. I simply sat back and basked in the moment of being around my girls. I didn't say much. I just wanted to hear everything they had to share.

While I was ashamed of my circumstances, they were all eager to share what had happened so far this year. Shannon's personal training business had picked up and she was contemplating quitting her "bills job"; Mia was ready to move from Columbus and back to Cincinnati to get a restart on her life with her own family; Janay was on the verge of celebrating a wedding anniversary and buying a home.

And me?

I was bipolar. I had been sent to hospital. I guess that's *something* to share with the group, but why? It didn't add to the quality of our conversation and it definitely didn't provide us with something to celebrate. I know I dwell on my diagnosis too much, but it's a part of me now. I can't not think about it. Every moment I'm questioning whether or not I'm experiencing mania or if I'm depressed or if I'm in a stable state. Lately, I cannot just *be*. And that is a hard pill to swallow.

"Drea, when are we getting copies of your book?" Shannon asked me in reference to the first book I published. I didn't have an answer. As much as I knew they were in my corner, I felt that business was business. If they wanted a book, they would have to buy it like everyone else. Is that rude? I turned and told her that it was available on Amazon and Kindle. She nodded and said that she would download it right now.

"Do you have a link or do I just search for it? What's the title?" *Oh my God. She's going to read it and know I'm crazy.* The book was titled, The Black Girl on Prozac. Couldn't get any more straightforward than that. I watched her as she typed the title into her phone. I could hear Janay and Mia's voices quiet in the background as my heartbeat came front and center. I took a deep breath.

"What's Prozac?" Janay asked innocently enough.

"It's an antidepressant I was on." I lowered my head ashamed my not so secret, secret had come out.

And almost as if in unison, the three of them let out a surprised "what?!"

"What?! You were taking an antidepressant? Why?" Mia interrogated me.

"Because I was depressed and I have anxiety." I let my lowered gaze meet hers and I forced a smile trying to make light of the situation. *Oh no.* I closed my eyes and lowered my head again. They all began to ask me questions about my prior diagnosis not really asking me much of anything. More or less, they were speaking amongst themselves and I just happened to be in the room.

I tried to zone them out until Shannon asked me, "so, how are you *now*?"

I knew it was coming. I wasn't as prepared

for it as I had thought. "Now…?" I paused. "I'm bipolar," I scoffed. "I'm on a different medication. I have to find a psychiatrist here so I can stay on track with everything and not bug out for no reason." I laughed and sighed. The looks on their faces were not ones of disgust or pity. They all genuinely looked concerned for me.

"What medication are you on and how long have you been depressed?" Mia questioned. She worked in a hospital, so she had some experience with mental health issues. She looked at me with squinted eyes.

"I've been depressed forever. Since like 7th, 8th grade. I'm on Abilify now."

"The anti*psychotic*?"

"Yes." *She knew. She knew how bad off I was.* I was humiliated at how easily my illness hijacked our enjoyable time together and conversations about their lives.

There was tension in the air. Once my book loaded onto Shannon's phone, she began reading. She remained silent. The book was my private diary that I just felt the need to publish. I figured that it was a start to the societal conversation about mental illness in African-

American women. Also, even if no one bought it, it gave me a sense of completion. Something I hadn't experienced in years.

I sighed. I excused myself from the group and headed upstairs to the bathroom. I wanted to cry so desperately. *I ruined a perfectly good trip and I didn't do anything but answer a few questions. I always ruin things.* I closed the door behind me and stared at myself in the mirror. I was being deprived of my tears. Whatever it was – my body, my eyes, my brain – I just could not cry.

I could hear everyone talking downstairs, including the boys as they found more toys to play with. *They are talking about me and I have no idea what they are saying. Why did I leave?* That was one of my biggest anxiety triggers – having people talk about me. It didn't matter if what they were saying was positive or negative, it was all bad in my mind.

Janay called from downstairs, "are you alright, Drea?"

I didn't answer. I just needed some time to breathe and process what was happening. I felt as though I was being attacked although I knew I wasn't. These women were my sisters and they had my best interest at heart. They just wanted to know if I was okay. My fight or flight response was officially on blast off mode. My heart began racing and beating like I had just ran up the stairs in a New York City high rise building with no elevator. My breathing was shallow and I was ready to go. I knew I was in a safe place, but I was thinking that everything about this situation was all wrong.

"Drea?" She called for me once more.

I wanted to slit my wrists. I hated when people shouted my name. I absolutely detested it. Again, I knew she meant well, but I thought I was being attacked. I took several deep belly breaths and tried to calm down.

"Give her some time," I heard Mia say from downstairs.

I shut my eyes and just tried to breathe normally. For something we do unconsciously so easily, it felt challenging to me. I was irritated with myself. I was frustrated with the situation. I was just so over it all. My eyes opened and I saw my reflection glaring back at me. I was mad at myself for not keeping my cool. I shook my head and claimed defeat. I opened the bathroom door and walked back downstairs.

Before I turned towards everyone, I faked

my smile and was met with Shannon's, "are you okay?" Wrought with unease, everyone just looked at me waiting for an explanation.

"Yeah, I'm good. Sometimes I just need a moment to recollect myself. But, I'm okay. I promise." I took a long sip of my wine before sitting back down. "Can we just not talk about this right now?" I asked seeking refuge at the bottom of my glass.

Chapter 3

4am met me in my own bed back in Atlanta. I was glad I had the chance to see my friends, but I was elated to be home. At least for now. The time for my move was swiftly creeping up on me and I just couldn't wait. My room was dark and a soft breeze came through my slightly opened window. I was wide awake and ready to start my day. After returning from the bathroom, I turned on the bedroom light. My cat just gave me that "*what-thee-eff-are-you-doing?*" look that I knew all too well. I ignored it and told him good morning as I pet him on his head.

The thing about mania – my mania – is that I never know when it is coming. My mixed and stable states are so similar that there is no warning. I literally wake up one morning and I am manic.

"Today is gonna be a good day," I said in a low sing-song voice as to not disturb anyone else in the house. I was ready to do something productive, but what? *I'm gonna rearrange my room!* I thought to myself joyfully. I got to work immediately. Despite being 5'2", 120 pounds of skin and bones, and haven't done any form of exercise in years, I found it fit to move my large heavy furniture; alone. This felt way better than being depressed… at least I was doing something that didn't require me to lay in bed all day.

I underestimated the size and weight of everything. When I tried to move my queen sized bed from its location near the closet to its new place under the window, I was stuck. The oversized dresser prohibited the 90 degree turn of the mattress, so it had to be moved, as well. Running off of curated energy, I decided it would be the smartest idea to just move the dresser with the drawers still in it. After all, I only needed to budge it a few inches. Needless to say, that did not work.

"Ouch!" I yelled. I hurt my shoulder, but it was bearable. Nothing was stopping me from my task at hand. I removed one drawer and then two drawers. I tried moving it again to no avail. I removed a third drawer and tried shifting the dresser once more. I was determined to make this work. It was after 5am and I had the goal of being done by the time another person woke up. The dresser hardly moved, but alas! It did move! I sat on the ground and used leverage from the wall to push the dresser with my feet. I got it halfway through the door and just like that, I had all the space I needed to maneuver my bed to its preferred spot.

What am I even doing? I asked, knowing this wasn't *right*. I felt awesome and that was unlike me. I didn't care that it was still dark outside or that everyone in the house and neighborhood was asleep. At that moment I didn't care. Nothing mattered except me getting my room in order. It was like I had tunnel vision in my mind. I could only focus on getting my furniture how I wanted it. I felt no pain after straining my back trying to lift my bed. The sweat that trickled down my neck didn't bother me. And the fact that I still had to move my desk and the dresser didn't faze me. There were no breaks. I had to finish it all ASAP.

With everything in its rightful corner or along its ideal wall, I felt accomplished. Only an hour had passed and I did it all by myself. My cat hid under the bed, as per usual, so I was alone, but I had to celebrate. Only, I wanted to celebrate by vacuuming and washing my sheets. Unfortunately, everyone in the house was still deep in slumber. Instead, I headed downstairs and made myself a cup of green tea. As I waited for the water to boil on the stove, I questioned my reality: *Am I okay?*

I understood what *THEY* told me about bipolar disorder when I was in the hospital. Risk taking behaviors was something for me to look out for.

But in my mind, applying for credit cards and loans wasn't risky. It was me trying to build my credit and be responsible. The thing that took it overboard was whenever I was denied, I simply went to another website and tried again. I was determined to fix my credit by any means… apparently, except paying my bills on time.

I wasn't working, so, technically, I couldn't pay my bills, I could only spend the money I had on my credit cards at the time. I paid for trips out of town, bought new notebooks and expensive pens (because who didn't like pretty stationary?) and ate my credit away. There was nothing left, so I tried and tried again.

I decided to check my Capital One credit tracker and I stared at the number on my computer screen. **27**. Twenty-seven hard inquires on my credit report. Twenty-seven hard inquiries gathered in a week. I felt overwhelmed. *How could I do this?* For the next few weeks I fretfully logged on to every credit tracker website and watched my score drop drastically.

"I'm such a failure," I said to the computer screen. I knew better, yet I couldn't do better. It was all just impulse; a knee jerk reaction. *Keep applying, then I can spend once I get approved.* It was an evil way of thinking, but it was how *I* was thinking… for the past 3 days. I didn't want to buy anything in particular, I just wanted the security of knowing that I *could* spend the money *if* I wanted to. And I knew I would want to. It was a sick cycle I had gotten myself into.

"Just one more and I'll stop," I purposefully said out loud to make the thought real and to hold myself accountable for my actions. I typed in the browser of my HP laptop, *'creditone.com.'* According to Credit Karma, my odds for approval with them were "great" so I knew I had a good chance this time. Filling out the application, I felt a rush of excitement. Once I hit *submit*, I was left to watch the little blue circle swirl, letting me know that my application was being processed.

"Congratulations! You've been approved!" The words practically jumped off the screen and I was elated. *Goal accomplished.* With a reported $400 credit limit, it was more than enough to soothe my need to keep applying to credit card companies. I was finally satisfied. I smiled at myself for being patient and not stopping until I got what I wanted. If only I had this same mindset in other aspects of my life.

My manic states had become my good friends. They made me feel happy and excited for life. They also gave me focus and motivation; all things I've been lacking for a while. Celebrating my re-found focus, I decided (on a whim) to drop out of my MBA program and try to find something that fit better with me and my personality.

"Should I do Mental Health Counseling or MFT?" I asked my best male friend and roommate, James.

"I think you would be great at either one," he assured me. "They both sound better than MBA. I don't know why you decided to do that in the first place," he laughed, but I knew he was serious. My original motivation for doing the Masters of Business Administration was to learn everything I could about the world of business since I was an entrepreneur. It made sense at the time, but I couldn't get a grasp on the concepts. Plus, it didn't entertain me so I never wanted to study. Needless to say, I all but failed the classes I did take.

"I know. But I thought I was doing a good thing by going that route. I wanted to help with your business." James and I had started a social media consulting business. I wanted to do more than post statuses as a co-founder. I wanted to be a part of the *business* and actually contribute to the company. But, business, it just wasn't *my thing*.

"I'm leaning towards Mental Health Counseling because… Grady," I laughed. Since being sent to psych, I have laughed off the situation. I acknowledge that I have an illness, but I still find it funny (yet, traumatizing) that I was really a patient on the 13th floor. In jest, I said, "Only crazy people can understand other crazy people." James laughed and told me to do more research.

I was serious. I wanted to study something that spoke to who I am as a person and something I had some experience with. I need to be interested in the subject matter and the individual courses. I became overwhelmed thinking about it, but I figured I'd do what I do best: make comparison lists.

First, I had to find schools with one of the 2 programs. The short list included University of Cincinnati and Northern Kentucky University for Mental Health Counseling, and Walden University and Northcentral University for Marriage and Family Therapy. I then wrote down the length of the programs, which were all very comparable, the names/topics of the required courses, cost, and any other interesting information I thought would be relevant when making my decision.

They all seem so perfect, I thought as I looked over my notes with satisfaction. The programs were so similar in that I would be helping people no matter which school I chose, but they were so different in what they offered as an experience. Despite the quality of the curriculums, one school stood out above the rest due to their instant decision policy. Once I scanned my list once more, I knew I had to apply immediately.

It was 4 in the afternoon and I was ready to start the rest of my life, again. I returned to my laptop and typed the University's URL into the browser. I clicked to the online application and began putting in my info. When I finished, I stared at the *apply* button.

"This is it." I clicked the button and the page refreshed. That was it. My intent to move forward and change the course of my life had been sent into cyberspace for someone to evaluate and determine whether the story my application told was worthy of acceptance. I took a deep breath and sighed. I had done it. "Adventure time," I told myself and closed my eyes.

Within the next half-hour, my iPhone was ringing. It was a number I didn't recognize, but was compelled to answer it.

"Hello, this is Andrea," I spoke cheerfully into the phone.

"Hi," a strange voice said back. "I'm Doug calling from Northcentral University regarding your application."

Oh, wow. That was quick, I thought enthusiastically.

"Yes. I'm calling to ask you a few more questions and provide you with information about the University and our Marriage and Family Therapy program. Is this a good time to chat?"

"Of course it is," I responded, sitting up in my bed trying to sound calm and confident.

Doug went on and told me all about the school and the MFT curriculum. He explained how the internships and licensure processes would be and even gave me a rundown of the schedule of classes according to what I put as my desired specialization: Child and Adolescent Therapy. At this point, I was ready to begin classes immediately. When he asked me if I had any questions, I proceeded to inquire, "when do I start?"

It made him laugh into the phone. "Well, we have to accept you first and have you fill out a supplemental application. From there, you will speak with an enrollment specialist and have a Skype interview with the Dean. How does all that sound?"

It was all too good to be true. *Maybe it seemed so easy because I actually wanted to do it.* It was exactly what I was looking for and it all felt like it fell into my lap.

After answering a few questions, I hung up from Doug and received an immediate call from Jamie, my enrollment specialist. *This school moves mighty fast.*

"Hello?" I answered my phone.

"Good afternoon, this is Jamie calling from Northcentral University. I am looking to speak with Andrea Paul."

"This is she," I replied, moving from my comfortable spot on the bed.

"Great! I'm your enrollment specialist and it is my job to get you into NCU. I had a chance to speak with Doug and looked over your application, and it seems like you would be a great fit for NCU," she said with bubbling enthusiasm.

Duh, I'm great, my neurotic thoughts interrupted her spiel.

She continued, "I would like to schedule a Skype interview with you and the Dean of the college. How's Wednesday at 10am, your time?" The school is based in Arizona, so she had to be clear about the time difference.

"That works for me," I said as I took notes in my

fancy new notebook.

"Awesome!" She exclaimed and went on to explain more about the application and acceptance process. I listened intently and just as quickly as she called, she hung up.

I was more than excited. I was thrilled to have made a decision and took the first step in seeing it through. It was the first time in a long time that I had done something like this and it felt good.

Chapter 4

I went to see a primary care provider today. For whatever reason, my blood pressure was 140/113. I went because I had not been for a check-up in years, and figured it was time.

"Are you on any medications?" She asked me.

"Abilify. 5 milligrams," I answered her nonchalantly as she typed her notes into the computer.

Without looking up at me, she queried, "what was your mental health diagnosis?"

"Bipolar I," I said even more coolly.

"Really?" The nurse looked at me, searching my face for some sign of *crazy*. I hadn't remembered her name, but she spoke to me like she had known me for a while. "That's interesting. This may be bad to say, but I've had patients who had mental health issues and they were never as stable as you are. Just looking and interacting with you, I could never tell you were bipolar." I simply tilted my head waiting to hear more of a story. This lady liked to converse and I let her talk.

"I had one patient who had bipolar disorder and she was just all over the place." She used her hands to further describe how "all over the place" her patient was. She continued, "I love that you are so compliant!" She smiled and clasped her hands together. "Let me ask you, what makes you stick with taking your meds? Why are you so compliant compared to other patients? Are you always this stable?"

"Because," I paused. *Why was I so compliant?* "Because, I feel like I have to be. I feel like I'm always like this. This is my normal." I shrugged. I was really unsure as to what drove me to take my pills every day. I didn't have a clue why, but she seemed pleased with my answer and continued with her series of medical history questions. I responded to them unconsciously as I looked around the sterile exam room and pondered. *Why was I one of the seemingly few who decided that my mental health was important? Why was it a surprise that I was compliant? Why did I take this seriously? Was it that rare for mental health patients to take their meds regularly?*

After her round of questions, she just looked at me and said, "I'm very proud of you wanting to stay on your meds and wanting to continue your care even though you've moved. Most other people would just quit until *something* happened." She implied that I was a rare breed and that my behavior was to be praised.

As a wannabe doctor and future therapist, I knew that there would be some difficult patients and clients in my future who I would have to work with to the highest degree, but how she made it seem created a feeling of uncertainty within me. *Did I want to have to deal with people who didn't want to do as I suggested? Would I have to fire my future clients? Will the inability to comply leave me jaded and wanting to quit whatever profession I was in?* It was hard to hear that, but I felt ready and up for the challenge.

Once the nurse left the room to gather my paperwork, I sat on the exam table a bit distressed. I had to tell her I needed a refill on my Abilify, but I didn't want to take it anymore. I wanted to be the non-compliant one for a change. Not out of defiance, but because I felt stable enough to not need it, even though I knew I did. When she returned, I knew I had to tell her.

"I need a refill on the Abilify because I took

my last pill last night. How would you suggest I go about getting that since I had the prescription written in Georgia?"

"Oh." She was taken aback. We both thought the appointment was over. She had done my physical, brought my paperwork, had a medical assistant come to give me a tetanus shot, and was sending me to the lab to have my blood drawn for testing. We were both just about ready to go. "I can give you a referral for mental health services here in the city, but I will be honest with you. It may be a while before you get in to see a provider. We just don't have that many mental health care professionals in Cincinnati."

I became worried. How could a place that was home to 3 or 4 hospitals within walking distance of each other, including a teaching institution, a medical school, and the department of health, not have enough providers for the city? It didn't make sense to me, but it was what it was. I would just have to wait.

"What could happen is, you could call your psychiatrist in Atlanta and have them call in a prescription here. If he doesn't do it, call me and I can write you a one month prescription for until you can get in with someone here," she said sincerely.

I took a deep belly breath. I was relieved I had options now. I thanked her.

"Is there anything else?"

"No. That's all," I smiled and thanked her again. And with that, she opened the door to escort me to the lab.

After having my blood drawn, I left the office and waited for Shannon to pick me up. While I sat in the waiting area, I called CVS to inquire about the cash price for a 30-day supply of generic Abilify.

"It's $800," the voice on the other end of the phone said.

I scoffed. "Are you serious? For the generic?" I couldn't believe what the pharmacy tech just told me.

"No, it's $800 for the brand name. There is no generic. It's fairly new, so the price is way up there."

"Ok. Thank you for the information." I hung up the phone not waiting for his response.

Wow. Eight-hundred-DOLLARS?! This illness was about to cost me the same amount as someone's rent payment every month. This fueled my want to stop taking it. *At Grady, I was getting the pills for free. How could I come here and pay $800?? If I absolutely needed to, how would I even afford it?* I couldn't. I have no money… Literally, none.

I called James and asked him to look up some info on another pharmacy's website on his computer since I could only see their mobile site from my phone.

"Can you go to the link I sent you on Facebook and see if Abilify is on their $4 list?"

"Ok. Hang on one sec. I'll text you with what I find," he said. James was always reliant and I owed him everything. Not to go into too much detail, but he helped me when I felt like I had no one in my corner. He was there when I broke down and couldn't see the light at the end of the tunnel.

"Thank you. I really appreciate it," I told him.

Within 2 minutes, I received his text. *"It's not there."* This meant that it would be almost – if not – impossible for me to get the medication ever again. Especially, without insurance.

"What am I going to do?" I whispered to myself in the hallway.

I texted James and told him what the guy from CVS said. *"It costs $800."* I put my phone away and looked out of the clinic's sliding doors. I just wanted to get back to the house and sleep. I have a job interview at 4:30 and wanted to be rested for it while I took some time to reflect on my current situation.

I couldn't help myself, James was my in-house counselor, so I had to tell him what I was thinking. *"Guess I won't be taking it,"* I texted.

"Can I pick it up?"

"Yeah. But I don't want it. LOL"

"Oh, ok. You're gonna try without it?"

"I want to try."

"Ok. Sounds like a plan."

"Is it an okay plan, tho?"

"Yup. Try until January. It's only two weeks."

"Okay."

Although he wasn't a doctor, he provided me with the confirmation I was looking for. *Everything would be alright, right?* If I have any episodes, whether depressive or manic, Shannon knows to take me to the hospital and James would send my medication right away. At least I had some type of system in place to handle what may come up. I was trying to be responsible and handle this the best way I knew how.

Still thinking about what the nurse said to me about being a great patient, I suddenly felt guilty. But, I was stable, so how bad could 2 weeks be?

I received my results from my lab work… Everything came back "perfect". The nurse called to personally tell me this morning and to remind me to get my psych meds. I only went to see her yesterday. Who knew lab results had only a 24-hour turnaround time? I still didn't want to get the Abilify, but she insisted.

"You're doing so well on it, I don't want you to have a relapse." That didn't freak me out… not at all. (Enter sarcasm.) *A relapse?* She said it like it was a bad thing. I was uber productive and focused during a manic episode. That wasn't bad at all. If anything, I saw it as a very good quality to have since I'm hardy ever so focused. *Let me have my relapse. It will only be for a short period of time.*

As for my job interview, I got it! I'm officially a working girl. While I am afraid of my "oh-I-don't-feel-like-going-to-work-today-so-I-won't" attitude, I think this change of pace will be good for me. Once I start, I'll have a set schedule to keep me on track, focused, and busy. But, we'll see.

Chapter 5

Mania has officially kicked in… I think. I started my new class last week and in terms of my focus, so-far-so-good. It actually has paid off. I completed 4 assignments in 2.5 hours. It's only 11:32am… Mind you, the syllabus said one of them would take five days to complete. *Is this mania or am I just super focused because I have nothing else to do at the moment?*

In reality, all of this is so confusing. It's really hard now. I didn't think I would say it, but I'm ready to get back on the Abilify. After so long of not taking it, I definitely felt a change in how I physically and mentally felt. I was in a good mood, but I was sleeping more. I knocked out assignments for school, which wasn't a good thing, in theory because "bulk uploads" weren't allowed, but hey, I got them done. I wanted to go shopping so bad. But, because I was still at Shannon's house with no car of my own to use, I was stuck inside trying to use my willpower to not whip out my new Victoria's Secret credit card and buy sweatpants I saw online that I thought were "so amazing". I began to get agitated (or is that cabin fever?). My energy was increasing and I couldn't channel it and I felt more aware and laser focused on tasks – whether productive or otherwise.

Since I submitted my assignments, I sat at my computer scrolling through Pinterest looking at images related to marriage and family therapy – and cute outfits. *I deserve a break. I did good today and the day has barely begun,* I thought to myself as I pinned a resource to my secret MFT board. This was to keep me from spending money and to give me a change of focus. Honestly, I'm not sure why I use Pinterest. I can't see myself going back to look at the pins and using them for reference in the future. I guess it's just something else to do.

As I tapped my foot on the wall while I sat at my desk, I couldn't help but let my mind wander. *Am I okay? Am I psyching myself out? How much longer can I go without the Abilify before I have a breakdown?* Taking my eyes away from my computer screen and pausing my tapping, I looked over to the stack of papers sitting next to me. It was all the resources the nurse gave me regarding psychiatry services in the area. Since I received the printouts, I hadn't read them, but now seemed like a good time. At least I decided to use my time to be productive instead of wasteful. (Look at me using what I've learned so far in my course's time management workshop! Manic much??)

A glance at the paperwork seemed overwhelming. For some reason, I couldn't get past the first page. This was strange. I just finished writing 6 pages of essays, completed a workbook, watched 6 videos, and did 2 discussion posts, but I couldn't read a simple pamphlet that could help me in the future. I immediately shut down. "What is *wrong* with me?" I questioned myself out loud. "I can't do this. I can't." It's so draining to go from "everything is awesome" a la The Lego Movie to "I don't want to do anything" within a 5 minute span of time.

…And I was doing so well...

What is life?

I feel miserable. I don't understand this feeling. I just don't. get. it.

I bought a car. A fairly new car with an astronomical monthly payment and high as ever insurance due to an "at-fault" accident I had in the past. I have a job. A job that I absolutely despise with long 10-hour days that I can't wait to leave. Oh! And I have an interview for the Mental Health Counseling graduate program I had been dreaming about. Just waiting to get in so I can complain about how hard the program is or how much it isn't what I thought it would be.

See what I did there? Everything good that I have in my life just has to be seen in a negative light. Everything. I mean, I have a new car after driving mine for almost 10 years! I have a job that pays me the most I've ever gotten paid—with benefits! I was chosen to interview for a competitive graduate program where I would be studying to help people like myself for the rest of my life, if I choose! These are all amazing accomplishments that I can't see nor accept for the life of me. All I can fathom is how bad it all is or can be.

I went from "*I need a new car because my car is on its last leg and I'm so excited to be able to purchase one*" to "*what is life even? This was a bad idea.*" I have the means to pay for the car through the full-time job I have that I get to in the new car. Ideally, the purchase was totally worth it. It was something I needed and I love the car. I just can't let that be the umbrella feeling that I have towards the situation. It's something I've done for a while, so it's not surprising now that I can verbalize that I recognize it.

Everyone says my feelings and thoughts are normal. "Everyone feels like you do," they say. How can this be normal? How can switching between the two ends of the spectrum—optimism and pessimism—at any moment's notice be normal? How can I make the decision to buy a car the same day that I go out and actually buy the car. No research. No savings. No preparation. How can I ask the Universe for a full-time job that allows me to pay my bills and live and then hate what is offered to me? How can I move to a different city and expect things to be great then wallow because I want to go back home? I just need some type of balance in my thoughts... a happy medium because the intrusive thoughts and risky decision making is not normal. It's simply not healthy.

I'm still faithfully taking my medication but I don't think it's working anymore. I cry all the time because I feel unhappy in life. I just want things to go according to a plan and be perfect so I can accept it all. But no. My emotions take over and all of a sudden I am screaming at myself and holding myself back from slitting my wrists. Whenever I get into a mood, I want to drive myself to the hospital because I feel unsafe. I want to be given a different medication and be someone's experiment, even for one night. When I finally dry my tears and breathe, I realize that this nightmare I've thought up is my reality and that things could be so much worse. I have to convince myself that I am indeed living a good life and that I should be grateful for my experience.

Currently, I'm in this mixed mental state that confuses me. That's all this is. *Right?* How do I come out of the pessimistic ideology I'm holding on to and go back to being optimistic and normal? I hate feeling stuck in this space, helpless and hopeless.

I finally ended up biting the bullet and went to one of the psych agencies my primary care nurse gave me the informational pamphlets for. Unfortunately, I wasn't able to meet with someone the day I went, but I was given an appointment for two weeks from now. I don't know if I'm glad to finally see someone or if I'm scared of what they will say about my "progress".

I walked into the large sterile building and approached the glass enclosed front desk.

"Hello?" I was greeted by the older black woman wearing a telephone headset as she lifted only her eyes from her computer screen.

"Uh, yes," I stuttered. "I'm here for, um, new intake and I'm unsure of where to go."

"Second floor," the lady said as she returned her gaze to the computer in front of her with no apparent regard for customer service.

"Thank you," I said with a smile and walked towards the elevator. I heard her mumble a quiet *"mmm-hmm"* when I pushed the elevator button with my back turned to her. *What was she thinking?* To her, was I crazy? I'm in a city that wasn't too racially diverse, so was it strange to see a black girl come in for treatment? Or was her utterance indication that I was, yet, *another* crazy black girl to be seen by her? I didn't know what to make of it. As the elevator doors opened and I stepped inside, I let out the breath I was unconsciously holding. I pushed the button for the second floor and closed my eyes as the doors closed in front of me. I had to know what that lady was thinking about me. That's my thing— people's reactions make me feel as though they are thinking something that I need to know. I know that it is irrational, but I can't seem to get past the uneasiness I feel in this uncomfortable situation.

The elevator doors opened once more and I stepped out. I walked to the left and was greeted this time with a smile from the woman at this glass surrounded desk.

"Hi. Welcome to behavioral services. How can I help you?" The woman asked through the circle cutout in the glass.

"I wanted to do a new intake," I said unsurely. I never know what to say in these situations where my request makes sense.

"Sure, no problem. Just fill these out for me and I will put you in the system. Unfortunately, you won't be able to see someone today." She handed me the clipboard through the slot over her desk and sent me to have a seat.

Drea, it's okay. Calm down. Just breathe.

I was nervous. I had forgotten about the woman downstairs and was overwhelmed with a new sense of anguish. I sat in a chair and placed the clipboard, my wallet, and phone in my lap. I let out a deep breath. I picked up the pen and began to write my full name on the form. I took another deep breath and continued. Date of birth. Address. Telephone number. I finished the first page. I placed the sheet of paper on the chair to the right of me and glanced over the mental health history form.

"In the past 2 weeks have you: felt down or blue most days? Had little interest in things you were once interested in?" The list continued...

70

"Have you had thoughts of harming yourself or others? Spent money you did not have?" I was selecting "most days" or "often" for a majority of items on the last two pages of the packet. By the looks of things on this paper, I needed to see someone ASAP. There was no questioning it. Once I completed all the forms, I looked them over, making sure I answered all the questions. I returned the clipboard to the woman behind the glass with a forced smile and returned to my seat. My not so distant future was uncertain. I didn't know if there would be some sense of urgency in my case because of how I answered the questions. Plus, the lady never asked me if I was seeking psychiatric or counseling services. *How would she know? Should I go back up there and ask what services this place provided? Should I tell her I needed both?* I just sat there staring at the television thinking of everything I coulda shoulda woulda said.

And I sat there. And I waited.

I watched people come out from behind the electric door that you needed an ID card to swipe in and out of. I watched bits and pieces of the news program that was on the TV mounted in the corner of the waiting area… There was another fire somewhere and some people were injured. My mind was just there, floating in its own space not paying attention to anything while paying attention to everything. I fidgeted with my keys. I crossed my legs. I turned to look out of the window behind me.

What is taking so long? I thought to myself. I was getting restless. The woman behind the glass who was initially so welcoming became indifferent in my mind while I sat there. She didn't care that I needed to see someone. She didn't care about my problems. In that moment, she cared about the cake her co-worker was showing her that was available in the back room. The two chatted and laughed for what seemed like 10 minutes and I just sat there.

Lost in my thoughts of observing the chipped paint on the wall next to me and the stained chair across from me, I didn't notice the lady behind the glass wave at me.

"Miss?" the woman sitting two seats away brought me out of my trance and she pointed to the window. I smiled and nodded at her.

"Thank you." I walked across the aisle and up to the window nervous of what she may say. Full of anxiety, I dreaded the short 5 step trek to find out what my forms had translated to.

"Here is your appointment: March 21st at

2pm." It was written on the back of the business card she handed to me through the slot in the window.

The 21st?! That was two weeks away and I felt as though I was on the brink of a slight breakdown. "Is that the earliest appointment to see someone?" I asked. I don't know where my voice came from since I was in shock by what she said. I started shaking a little. My face felt flushed. My hands became hot. The anxiety was taking over my body and I was uncertain of what to do at that moment. Fight or flight.

I asked again, "That's the earliest available?" I looked at her as if she lied to me.

"Yes ma'am. That is the soonest appointment I have available." She kept her warm demeanor, but it was stern. She meant it and there was nothing I could say or a different way I could ask the same question to change the facts she presented.

"Okay." I felt defeated. "Thank you." I looked at the card and turned towards the elevators with my head low. As I walked away I turned back and told her to have a good day. She smiled. I pushed the button for the elevator and waited. My hands were still hot and my body tensed to stop the trembling. I stood there and waited. My anxiety flooded my body once again as I watched the doors open and there was a car full of people just looking at me, waiting for me to get in the elevator so they could go on about their business. I looked down and entered the car. I peeked around the man standing in the corner to see if the button for the first floor was lit. *Of course someone pushed it. Duh, Drea. We're only on the second floor. Everyone here has to exit on the first if they are still on the elevator.* Common sense kicked in, but it was cruel and made me uncomfortable. Yup, even more uncomfortable than I already was. I forced to make myself small in the crowed space and just stared at my phone's home screen to make the time for the short ride a bit more bearable.

Once I was off the elevator and back in the main lobby, I deflated. I was so tense, I hadn't realized that I was holding my breath. I let out a sigh. I walked out of the building right into the middle of a crowd that had congregated in front of the door.

"Excuse me," I said in barely a whisper. I maneuvered my way between the people and made my way straight to my car. But, it wasn't my car I made it to. I forgot that I had bought a new car and that it was waiting for me on the other side of the packed parking lot. My little blue Nissan was no longer and I had to search for the green Mazda in the sea of green cars. I was frustrated. I felt as though I was going to faint and I needed to get home ASAP. I pulled out my keys and pressed the lock button to find the car. I heard it beep and I speed walked towards it. I unlocked the door and got inside. I was finally safe from the outside world. This cocoon of sorts was my temporary safe haven until I earned myself a safe breathing rhythm and a relaxed body position.

I sighed and deflated once more. I closed my eyes, dropped the business card the lady handed to me into the cup holder, gripped the steering wheel, and just breathed. I couldn't control myself. My body immediately went rigid again and my breathing stopped. No matter how many times I tried to relax, it didn't help. I wanted to put my face in my hands and start crying. Unfortunately, there were no tears. There was nothing to relieve the stress I felt except time. I just had to wait it out. *Why did I feel this way?* I didn't have an explanation. My body became hot, my heart was beating hard, and I began to shake more violently than before. It was making me mad. Whenever I get to this point, I get really scared. I want to scream. I want to cry. I want to slit my wrists. I want to just calm down.

It's okay. I still hadn't opened my eyes. I instructed my body to stop shaking and to start deep breathing. That made me tense up even more. *What was wrong with me? What was happening to me? Should I go to the hospital?* "It's just too much stimulation," I reasoned. I opened my eyes and realized that I was grabbing the steering wheel so hard, my hands began to cramp. I released my death grip and dropped my hands into my lap. I forced my breathing and pushed the button to start the car. "I have to go, now," I told myself. I felt nothing, yet I felt everything. I just knew that I was going to flip out at any moment and I needed to be home—safe—to do it.

In the five minutes it took to get to the house, I finally calmed down. Driving put me in a state I recognized, yet couldn't put my finger on. I relaxed and made it safely to my parking spot in the backyard. I pushed the button to turn the car off and I sat there for a moment not thinking of anything, just watching the breeze blow the branches in front of me. My heart rate and breathing slowed and I felt as though I could move voluntarily again. I grabbed my wallet and got out of the car. The same light breeze that made the branches dance, touched my face and I embraced it. I was okay now and I could make it through the rest of the day—hopefully.

Chapter 6

"I hate this! I hate all of this! What am I even doing?! This was a bad idea!" I screamed into the phone. "I can't do it. I'm ready to come home."

I called James and needed to vent about my new, adult life. My job, that I specifically hated, had spurred something in me that I hadn't felt before—hate. I absolutely hated my job and how my life was going. I was ready to go back to Atlanta and try my hand at entrepreneurship again. My eyes began to tear up. I was sad and conflicted. I knew I had responsibilities both to life and myself but I just wanted to curl up in a ball and sob (or sleep) my days away. You know when they say that you don't know what you have until it's gone? That is so true. I didn't realize how great my life was before. Now that I'm not living the way I used to and experiencing the things I want to, it all means nothing now. I'm living a great big ball of nothing meaningful. Crying myself to bed every night isn't allowing me to write a book or find a job I love. Crying every night gives me nothing and I know that.

"No," he said sharply. "You're making so much progress in Cincinnati that if you come back all of that work will mean nothing."

"Just like my life," I said in return under my breath. To any sane person who didn't know me would think this was the beginning of my suicidal thoughts. Little would they know that I was deep into my feelings and had already plotted on how I would do *it*. I would do it in a very anticlimactic way. I would simply slit my wrists and allow myself to bleed out. I would want to suffer because it's what I think I deserved and would want someone to find me in a tub full of my own blood—just like in the movies. It would be only then that I would know if people truly cared. How? Because they would call my name and when I wouldn't answer they would come looking for me. Of course the last place they would look would be the bathtub because by now the house would have this air of haunting dismay. They would pull the curtain back and there I would be: sunken into the tub lifeless and pale. They would then swoop down into the tub and grab me, yelling my name, and shaking me. "Drea! Drea! Andrea!" There would be no response. They would then pull me out of the tub and lay me on the floor. At this point they are beyond freaking out and begin shaking me once more. A phone would conveniently be in their jeans pocket and they would call 911 as they sat on the floor next to me.

"9-1-1. What's your emergency?" The calm voice on the other end would ask."

"It-it's my friend. I, umm, just, uh, found her body in the, uh, bathtub," they would stutter in between sobs. They would provide the dispatcher with all of the necessary details and the story would end with me not actually dying but ending up in a mental facility left to speak with a psychiatrist everyday about how I'm feeling while I'm drugged up several types of medications...

Yes, I've thought about this... Or I've watched too many movies with a "mental" patient.

Despite all the details, I'm too much of a coward to actually do anything to harm myself in real life, but trust me, there's a plan in place, no matter how romanticized it is.

"I haven't made any progress!" I yelled into the phone at James. "I'm still the same person I was and I hate it. The only thing that has changed is that I don't sleep all day. Now I work instead. I'm still the same anxious, depressed, scared, bipolar girl I was when I left. Nothing has changed. I need the safety of home and I'm crying because

I can't get that."

I was emotional and finally had a reason for my emotions. I was disappointed in the route my life had taken. I watched social media way too closely and that took its toll on me. Everyone I knew was getting married, growing their families, working in careers they loved, and traveling the world, and here I was trying to figure out if I want a latte or cappuccino and where my dream life was. I was comparing myself and I knew it and I knew I shouldn't. *Don't compare yourself to others, Drea.* I knew better. But how could I not when it was always in my face every time I opened an app on my phone? It didn't matter if it was twitter, Facebook, Instagram, snapchat, or periscope… I was bombarded with everyone's ideal life and I felt stuck so far behind last place.

"I just can't." It was that simple. I was irritated and frustrated and I wanted to throw something with the intention to break it. In this moment there was nothing no one could say that would make me feel better about my own life's failure. It was always the same thing every time. I was irritated and wanted to be left alone for a few days then things would be better. It had been a week and nothing changed. I was still mad at the world and myself.

It was always like I was fighting some internal battle; I hated everything, then I suddenly loved everything. I can't control it and that is the hardest part of my day to day life. Sometimes there was a reason for my depression or anxiety, other times there was nothing to blame. It was just me. That's how I am.

After a long silence I told James that I would speak with him later and hung up the phone. I sat in my bed and cried. I didn't understand why tears were moving down my face, but they were. I did everything in my power to make them stop. Crying was full of discomfort for me. I saw it as a sign of weakness and that if I cried it meant something was truly wrong with me. I attempted to distract myself with the very thing that brought me here—a stint on social media. I needed to get out of my own head and do something passively for a while. I scrolled and I scrolled down every timeline and news feed I had on my iPhone. Facebook, Twitter, Instagram, Periscope, Snapchat, Pinterest, and Tumblr. It didn't help. An hour had passed and I was still crying, albeit, silently now, but the tears wouldn't stop. I inhaled deeply and let out a slow breath. I laid back onto my pillows and looked at the ceiling, glad I had a day off from work. There was no way I could function in this mindset. I had been wiping my eyes and face so hard, I'm sure I was as red as a beet by now. My cheeks were raw and my eyes felt puffy. I sniffled and closed my eyes. I felt unsafe. I had the energy to do something, but felt like doing nothing. I had all the thoughts, yet there was nothing I could make coherent. I tried to fall asleep, but my body wanted to move about.

Yet, another hour passed me by and I wondered where Shannon was. I needed to do *something* and I didn't care what I was at this point. She was at work and I knew that. She wouldn't return home until after 9pm that night so I was all alone left to fend for and take care of myself for another 9 hours. I became flushed and angry. There was something I was missing, but I had no idea what it was.

I threw the comforter off of my body and rose out of the bed. I grabbed my Converses and put them on my feet. I took my time with tying them because I didn't know where I was going. I took my jacket off of my chair and gripped my purse. I felt my pockets to make sure I had cash and my keys and I took off out of my room and down the stairs. I sat in my car with no plan. Where was I going to go? I had lived in Cincinnati before, but I never got to know the city. I didn't know where a good look out spot was or a nice little coffee shop. Nonetheless, I pulled out of the long driveway and just started driving.

236 miles. That's what the dashboard read. Where could I go with 200 miles worth of gas? I didn't know. I made my way downtown and drove between the plethora of office buildings and people walking to and fro on their lunch breaks. Everyone moved with authority and purpose. They had places to be and they were getting there. Then there was me; lost in the crowd trying to find somewhere to go. Lost in the sea of commuters, I had the idea to drive towards University of Cincinnati's campus. I hadn't been in the area since I left Cincy in 2010, so it would be nice to see something familiar. I pulled over and took my phone from its place in the cup holder. I pressed the button for the Google Maps app and typed *University of Cincinnati* in the search bar. There it was; good old Clifton.

The voice came through the speakers of the car, "Turn right." I obliged. "Continue for one and a half miles." I obeyed the direction. Once I reached McMillian Street it was all muscle memory. I turned off the GPS and just wandered around the campus. Nothing was the same, nothing was even similar or noticeable. This wasn't the experience I came here to have.

"Wow," I said in a whisper to myself, in awe of what I did see. Calhoun Street had become an oasis and the epitome of a college campus. There were restaurants and yoga studios everywhere. There was a Starbucks. There wasn't a shortage of new apartments in sight. Things had really developed a lot from when I was student. The once dismal street was now bustling with lively college students walking from their fancy apartments to class. This was a different world. Different than what I had once known. I turned right down Clifton and expected much of the same. Here, nothing had changed and I felt my anxiety ease. I zoned out and allowed myself to just drive. Stopping at a long red light brought me back to reality and by now, I had made a complete circle around the school.

By now I would have thought that I would have felt better by getting out of the house and going for a drive, but that wasn't the case. I was still irritable and every brake light I saw flicker while we had the right of way with a green light, made me mad all over again. My body was tense and I had no control of my breathing. I finally made a decision on where to go… The hospital. This had gone on long enough and it was my fault. I hadn't taken my medicine for a few weeks and I allowed everything to bother me. But, now, I could no longer control what was happening. I headed down MLK Drive and turned onto a side street into the large parking deck in front of the emergency entrance. I took a ticket from the machine and weaved through the lot looking for a parking spot. *It can't be this packed on a Wednesday...* I guess people are sick every day so it doesn't matter what day it was. I digressed.

I finally found a spot towards the back of the parking deck and got out of the car. I sighed. My heart was beating so hard. I was scared. Scared of what would happen and what they would say. *Would they make me stay overnight? Would it be as intense as my experience at Grady Hospital?* I was unsure and that scared me. I walked to the stairs and went down two flights. Reaching the bottom, I was met by a woman pushing a stroller and a small child racing to keep up behind her. I smiled and paused and let them pass me. The woman looked disheveled and tired. They, too, were headed towards the emergency room entrance. I walked slowly and kept my head down. The sliding doors greeted me and I was beyond anxious. I followed the signs for the emergency waiting area. Once I got there, the space was filled with an overwhelming emptiness. The only people in the waiting room was an older gentleman in a wheelchair, half asleep, and the mother with her two children that passed me on the way in.

"Welcome to University Hospital. How can I help you?" The nurse asked me from behind her station at the main desk. I was confused. How could this large, urban, research hospital have an empty ER? I looked behind me to make sure I hadn't missed a sign pointing in a different direction. Clearly not amused by my confusion, the nurse asked again, "how may I help you?" This time with an air of attitude.

I turned my attention towards her. "I'm looking to see someone in psych. I'm currently experiencing symptoms and just want to check and see if I'm okay."

"What are you experiencing?"

"Umm… irritability, I'm very emotional, I feel like I have a lot of energy I can't release, and in short, uh, I feel like I might harm myself," I admitted to her through my stutters. I chuckled under my breath and shook my head because I sounded so ridiculous.

Her demeanor changed. She was concerned. "Do you feel like taking your life?"

"No, not at all. Just want to feel something… so more along the lines of cutting myself opposed to dying. I haven't attempted anything." I chuckled again trying to make light of the situation. But I made it to the hospital. There's not too much "light" I could get out of it at this point.

"Have you been diagnosed with anything prior?" She asked looking up at me.

"Yes. I have been diagnosed with bipolar disorder and have been on medication for it."

She nodded and asked me my name, birthdate ,and social security number, and if I had any allergies and typed the information into her computer. I fidgeted while I stood there. I don't understand how I was so comfortable offering up so much information at once. I was anxious, yes, but it all flowed out of me with no effort on my part. She rose from her chair and went over to the printer to gather my plastic bracelet. This all felt too familiar. Next, she asked me to come around the desk and sit in a chair so she could take my vital signs.

"Your blood pressure is a little elevated," she said.

"It's always high. I'm on medication for it. It runs in my family."

"What medications are you taking currently?"

"Abilify, 5 milligrams, and a diuretic for my blood pressure." She made a note of it and continued her questions.

"Do you smoke or drink? Have you used recreational drugs? Have you taken prescription drugs that weren't yours? Are you seeing or hearing things other people can't hear or see?"

Honestly, I answered the questions without thinking. I stared at the flower pattern on her scrubs and followed the vine up to where her badge was clipped. "No. No. And no."

"How are you feeling now? You seem fine."

"Yeah... I'm not though. I feel so overwhelmed right now. I just want to sleep."

"Do you want to sleep and never wake up?" A question I was all too familiar with. It was a question my psychologist always asked me when I told her I just wanted to sleep.

"No. I just want to nap the feeling away and go back to normal."

"I understand." Before she could finish her thought, another nurse came through the huge double doors leading to the back. The nurse I was working with told the new nurse, "Ms. Paul here needs to see psych this afternoon."

The new nurse seemed to be unfazed. I assumed that a statement like that warranted some type of empathy or at least a facial expression. I got nothing from her but a simple smile and an "okay."

"Nurse Bethany here will take you to the back." And just like that, Bethany escorted me through the wooden double doors she came from.

"Thank you," I tried to call back to the first nurse, but I'm sure the doors closed my voice in and she didn't hear me. I was led, in silence, down a long hallway. So far this was nothing like my Grady experience. There was no stretcher, no policemen, no screaming patients… The place looked sterile and was relatively empty except for the few nurses and doctors I saw pass us by.

"Have a seat in here and Dr. Johnson will be with you shortly." Bethany finally acknowledged me on our walk. My shoulders were tense and I was just about ready to go home, but I knew I needed to be seen. I was here, so it was time to get it over with.

That was easier said than done. I waited in

the room Bethany put me in for over an hour. Nervous to step out of the room to flag someone down, I just sat there on the bed, waiting. At least I had my phone (and charger) to keep me company through it all. The time passed slowly and right when I mustered enough courage to get up and ask where the restroom was located, a bald, middle aged man in a soft yellow shirt and tie entered my room.

"Hello, Ms. Paul, I'm Doctor Johnson," he reached his hand out to shake mine without looking up from his phone. I obliged. Once his gaze finally met my own, he seemed a little surprised to see *me. Yes. I'm your patient; a seemingly sane black girl. Please treat me appropriately.* It's always so nerve-wrecking to have people perceive your presence as strange when they find out you have a mental illness. He was a psychiatrist, yet he was uncertain about how to react towards me, a psychiatric patient. "I hear you're not doing too well today. Tell me about it," he said as he sat down in the chair next to the bed, staring at me.

I turned to look at him. "I'm just not feeling *normal.* I didn't know what else to do besides come here." He just looked on. "I feel irritable, I have a lot of energy I can't release, and I want to cut myself. Not really, but it feels that way. I haven't done anything though."

"I see. And you have been diagnosed as bipolar, correct?"

"Correct."

"Have you been taking your medication as you're supposed to?"

I lied, "yes. I take it at night and it makes me fall asleep."

He took a brief note in the pad that was in his hands and returned his attention to me. "What are you on?"

"Abilify, 5 milligrams."

"How long were you on it?"

"Uh… Since November, maybe. But, before that, I was on Prozac 20 for depression and anxiety. That was since last summer."

He went back to writing his notes. "Are you seeing or hearing things that aren't there?"

"No," I answered. I was getting frustrated because all this was answered already. He could read my chart and get the info. *Why was he asking me this again?* "I just feel overwhelmed. I'm tense all the time, I have all this energy, yet

I want to sleep all the time, I'm always upset. Normally I'm very positive and upbeat, but now I'm down and pessimistic. My depression is more standard for depression: I'm sad, anxious, I don't want to do anything and I sleep all the time. This is a different feeling for me," I tried to explain in depth to limit his questions.

Here I go again. This is what happened at Grady. I kept talking and they felt the need to keep me overnight. If I do that here, they will keep me again. I don't want to stay here tonight and I have to work tomorrow.

I stopped speaking and put my head down. I didn't want him to think I was ready to be admitted. I just needed answers to how I was feeling. He continued to write.

"Hmmm," he uttered.

What is 'hmmm'??? Why did he do that? What does it mean?

"What does that mean?" I blurted out, surprised at myself.

The doctor looked up from his pad a little taken aback at my abruptness. "Well, umm," he stuttered. "I'm considering keeping you here overnight for observation."

I took a deep breath and nodded. Medically, I understood. Realistically, I didn't want it to happen. "I have to be at work tomorrow," I said as though it would stop him from keeping me. I was beginning to feel uneasy. Something wasn't quite right with me in that moment. Like all of the feelings I had been having up until that moment, I couldn't place what I was experiencing within my mind and body.

"I see. I'll go consult with a colleague and come back with a plan for you. It shouldn't take long," he said rising out of his seat. And with that, he left me alone.

Chapter 7

"No! I want to go home!" I yelled at the
nurse trying to give me my meds. "I pushed
her hand away from my face. I don't know how
long I've been here, but I wasn't having it any
longer. "Noooo!!" I screamed at the top of my
lungs and I walked to the opposite side of the
room. "I'm not going to take it," I claimed as
I crossed my arms over my doubled hospital
gown. I wasn't a threat, so they saw no reason to
subdue me, but I wish they had. I had begun to
have hallucinations and hated that I had to stay
in the hospital. I was scared of everyone and
everything because I couldn't tell if it was real or
not.

"Ms. Paul, you have to take these pills this
morning," the nurse said as she sat them on
the table near my bed. She was done with me
and my yelling. Wasn't she used to this by now?
Patients yelling and running away from her…
She had to be, right? She looked at me in my
eye, opened the door, and closed it behind her.
I was left in the corner of my room staring at
the little cup holding the two pills I was being
forced to take. Tears streamed down my face

as I stood there. I wiped my eyes with my right hand and returned to my crossed arm position. I couldn't move. Looking around the room, I noticed, for what felt like the first time, how sterile the place was. I blinked the tears back.

The walls were white, the blinds were white, the sheets were white, the floor was white... The only thing that was a stark difference was me. Here I was, this smart, pretty, put together black girl in this very white environment. *Why did I come here? What made me agree to being checked in?*

Honestly, I had no idea where I was and what the pills were. The last thing I remember was calling James and telling him I had checked myself into the hospital. Afterwards, I was transported to a nearby hospital that handled the psychiatric cases that came through the University's Hospital.

I was blinded by the water that welled in my eyes which I kept wiping away, but steadily came back. I unfolded my arms and walked over to the disheveled bed. I climbed in and covered my body with the thin blanket. I turned onto my side and continued to stare at the cup of pills. "What are they?" I asked myself. I reached for them and looked into the cup. I didn't recognize them. They were neither Prozac nor Abilify. I placed the cup back down. It was final. I wasn't taking the pills. At least not now. I closed my eyes and sighed.

I woke up to a knock at the door, I thought it was the nurse who tried to force me to take the pills earlier. It was lunch time and the dietician welcomed herself into my room. I quickly sat up on the bed anticipating having to fight my way past her. Paranoia had set in and I wasn't ready for it. What was happening? She smiled and I held my breath ready to swing my fists in her direction if she came at me. She placed the tray near the cup of pills and left the room. I let out my breath. I saw a shadow out of the corner of my eye and I turned my head to see what it was.

Nothing.

There was nothing to see except the coat hanger lodged in the corner of the room. I saw the flash again and turned in the opposite direction.

Nothing.

"What is wrong with me?!" I cried out loud in the silent room. *Was I seeing spirits or something?* I held my head in my hands and brought my knees to my chest. I was officially crazy. I was seeing things that weren't there and afraid people are out to hurt me. What made it even worse was that I recognized that this wasn't real. None of this was real. I was even more frightened and began to cry harder.

Another knock came to the door. I simply looked up, expecting the visitor to let themselves in like the girl had before them.

"Ann-dree-uh?" A man in a sweater vest and a thick European accent poked his head into my room.

"Aun-dre-yuh," I corrected him. I never correct people when they mispronounce my name. It had been that way since I was a child. I accepted the many ways *Andrea* could be pronounced and I answered to them all. Today was the day that didn't fly with me. How dare he come into my room, say my name incorrectly, *and* have on this Bill Cosby looking sweater? I was seething and I was ready to snap. "Are you my doctor?" I questioned him as he walked in with a medical student in tow. I saw his badge swing on his hip. *Charles Ricardi, D.O.* it read. It was like I was having an out of body experience, watching myself have this attitude that was so unlike me.

"Yes, I am. I am Dr. Ricardi. I have a medical

student here with me today, Student Dr. Samantha Walsh. She'll be observing."

I just looked at the med student. I hated her hair. Everything you thought about a psych med student is true. She had the over-sized glasses, her hair was red, curly, and unkempt, and she was short and stubby. I hated her. The poor girl hadn't spoken a word, yet, I hated her for being in the position I wanted to be in for so long. I wanted to go to medical school and pursue psychiatry since I loved psychology so much, but I couldn't pass organic chemistry to save my life. It was on to the next best thing since med school wasn't an option any longer. I hated her because she was on the path to becoming a doctor and for whatever reason, her glasses bothered me. They just didn't suit her. I wanted to smash her face in.

"Andrea? Did you hear me?" The doctor snapped me out of my trance.

I blinked and looked at him. I nodded. I had no clue what he said. But whatever it was, I agreed. Dr. Ricardi walked over to the table that housed the pills and my lunch and handed the little cup to me.

"Where did you go just now?"

"I'm not going to take them," I said ignoring his question.

"Why not, Andrea?"

"I'm afraid of not feeling anything and becoming a zombie. I don't want that. The Abilify was working just fine, give me that." With that, I saw another shadow cross the room. I jutted my head in its direction.

"What is it?" The doctor asked concerned. The med student turned to look at the door with me.

"It's nothing," I lied and the student turned her attention back to me and what the Doctor was saying.

"For the past few days you've been going through a psychosis episode and having paranoia. You were seeing things other people couldn't see and thought people were going to harm you. Do you remember this at all, Andrea?"

"What? I had a mental breakdown? Like for real?" I questioned him in awe at this new information. "What's today?" I asked. It wouldn't have mattered what he said because I didn't know what day I came in on.

"Today is Friday the…"

"How long have I been here?" I cut Samantha off.

"You've been here for 3 days," Dr. Ricardi said. "Do you know where you are?"

My face said it all. I had lost all track of time and I didn't even know it. How could this happen? I was no longer upset at the pair that stood in front of me; I was angry at myself for letting this happen. "What happened?" I asked quietly. I looked to Dr. Ricardi for solace, but all he had was bad news. Apparently I was manic when I was in the ER at University Hospital. When they transported me to Deaconess, I broke down. I had told them that there were voices everywhere and that if I walked in they would start attacking me. Coming up to my room, they gave me a dose of a sedative because I was fighting the patient transport volunteer. The next day, I walked up to the nurses' station and yelled that I was going to slit my wrists if I had to go to "the room with all the crazy people" because they scared me. Then, there was today. I was a little better, and finally lucid, so they decided to leave me be.

I just looked at him; looking for more to the story. Taking a deep breath, I inquired, "where is my phone?"

"All of your belongings are with security. You'll get it when you are discharged."

"When will I be discharged?"

"That is up to you. When you cooperate, take your medication, aren't having any more psychotic episodes, we can consider it."

"Consider it?! I need to leave now. I have to get to work. Plus, my family has no idea where I am! I need to get in contact with them!"

I pulled back the sheets and lunged for the door. Once I was in the hallway I didn't know where to go. The hall was never ending and there was no one in sight. I couldn't hear the telephones ringing and the monitors beeping. I turned right and started running. I was surprised the doctor didn't come after me. Each room I passed, the door was closed. What I failed to notice was the eerie quiet coming from everywhere. I had to question myself, *is this real?* How was I in a hospital and it be no hustle and bustle of nurses and doctors moving about? I stopped dead in my tracks and heard a voice ask, "what is it? Why did you stop?" I turned to meet the face of the person who was speaking to me, but like the shadows, I was met with nothing.

I held my breath. My eyes darted in every direction they could look. *What the hell was that? Where did it come from?* Iit wasn't inside my head. It wasn't a thought... I *heard* it. Now, I knew I was going delusional. The tears returned. I turned around and began walking back to my room. When I got there, the doctor and the med student were gone. I peered inside and started sobbing. I fell to the ground and let every emotion I felt out of my body through my tears. Barely 10 feet away from a bed, I curled up on the floor and just cried.

"Stop crying. No one cares," the voice whispered. I heard it loud and clear.

"This isn't real. This isn't real..." I cried into the tiled floor holding and shaking my head. "I can't take it."

"No one cares about you and what you feel," the female voice continued.

"Stop it! Stop it! Just stop!" I screamed loudly. I put my back against the wall and sat up. Bringing my knees to my chest and my hands to my ears there was nothing I could do but sit there and just rub my eyes with every tear that fell. The voice laughed.

After a few moments of silence, I got up and

went to lay in the bed. I saw the cup with the pills looking at me lying there, helpless. I picked it up and looked inside. The two pills were still unfamiliar, but I knew it was now or never. I had to make all of this stop. I sat up and took the cover off the lunch that had been prepared for me. Underneath, was a cranberry juice box. I grabbed it from the plate and replaced the cover, totally ignoring the mush that was beside it. I poured the pills in my hand and threw them to the back of my throat. I quickly followed up with the juice. I swallowed, hard, trying to will the voice and hallucination away. I laid back down wondering how long this will last. Soon after, I was asleep.

Looking around the room I felt light. To my right was a lady eating her hair and a large screen television on some courtroom show and to my left opened a large room holding 10 or so other patients either playing cards or standing around speaking to each other or themselves. I was in a daze and I knew it was from the pills. Everything seemed back to normal, but I was foggy. I felt slow and lethargic as if I was drunk off a bottle of moscato wine. Everything I did felt delayed and I was emotionless. After crying for what seemed like ages, feeling nothing was an unwelcomed existence. Nothing stimulated me. I just sat there staring out the window. Trees, a parking lot, and short road made up my view. Unless you were close enough or facing downtown Cincinnati, there was nothing to see, yet I was either fascinated or forced with looking out the window. I couldn't move myself away. Television was of no interest and I didn't want to interact with the other patients.

"Ms. Paul?" It was the nurse from this morning. *Was it this morning or the morning before?* I didn't keep track of the days so I had no idea where I was in the week. I knew I was fired from my job by now, so, it didn't matter.

I blinked slowly and answered without breaking my gaze through the glass, "Huh?"

"It's time to go see the doctor," she said in a calm voice. At least it was calmer than when I last saw her. She touched my arm and I pulled away. She was out to get me and I knew it. She was being nice as she waited for the perfect moment to strike. She was drugging me so I wouldn't be able to fight back when the time came. I squinted my eyes at her trying to read her face.

Drea, this is stupid. You're not crazy. This isn't you. Try to calm down so you can go home.

Another voice in my head caught my attention. I couldn't tell if it was me or that other one I had been hearing lately telling me to kill myself. The words weren't hostile this time, but I couldn't decipher it. I rose up out of my seat and let the nurse lead the way. This would be the first time—at least the first time I recognized—going into a doctor's office. After taking the elevator to the 16th floor, the nurse led me down an unfamiliar hallway and tapped at a door next to Van Gogh's The Starry Night painting. *How appropriate,* I thought.

"Come in," a voice came from inside the office. The nurse opened the door and there sat Dr. Ricardi. He stood behind his desk waiting for me to make my way into the room. I was nervous. I looked to the floor for solace. The last time I saw him, I had a total meltdown, was in a maze, and heard voices. I didn't know what to expect this time and that freaked me out. I held my breath and walked in, hesitantly. "Andrea!" he exclaimed as though he should have greeted me with a hug. He pronounced my name correctly and I darted my eyes at him without raising my head and crossed my arms. I inhaled sharply and slowly walked towards the chair facing him. The nervousness didn't leave my body. I sat in the oversized chair and looked around. The nurse closed the door and left us alone.

The room didn't fit the look of the modernized hospital. It was lined with ornate bookcases full of books on psychiatry and the human mind. The large window had a red velvet curtain tied on each side, allowing the sunlight to ease its way in. By now, the Doctor was speaking to me and I completely zoned him out. I was too busy observing my surroundings. The floor was graced with a decorative rug with tassels on each end... A sure tripping hazard. Dr. Ricardi's wood desk was a thing straight from the Antique Roadshow, having been no younger than 100 years old with its intricate carvings and bulky wooden legs. It must have weighed a ton and took six men to transport it into the hospital. The room itself was dark and mysterious like a room in an old castle-like house on a hill. How did he accomplish this feel in a hospital?

Dr. Ricardi was still speaking and I was catching every other word. "Psychosis... paranoia... bipolar... antipsychotic." He went on and I settled in the chair. I brought my left hand to my mouth and bit the tip of my thumb. I already knew it, I was crazy and I was getting crazier by the day. I was ready to go home and go back to my normal life.

"What do I have to do to get out of here?" I asked, interrupting his spiel.

Taken aback, he answered simply, "get better."

"Can I call my family? I haven't spoken to them since I got here."

"Yes. Certainly. You will have to see the nurse about your phone privileges."

I paused. "How do I just get better?"

The Doctor took a moment. "Take your medications, go to therapy, get better. We are waiting to see how long this cycle will last."

"Cycle? Like my manic-depressive cycle?" I had read about bipolar disorder when I was diagnosed and learned what I could about it. I shifted in my chair to turn towards Dr. Ricardi who was now by the window. The view from his office was much better than the group room. While it wasn't the city view I longed for, it was a nice one. The tree cover looked as though it went on for miles and miles… as though we were right in the middle of a forest. I began playing with my hair which was all over my head by now, I'm sure. "How long can it last?" I questioned nervously.

"Studies have shown," he began, "that a

cycle can last an average of 13 weeks." He let out a cough. "We just want to make sure your depressive state isn't as severe as your mania."

"Excuse me? 13 weeks?! Are you serious?!" I didn't move from my place in the chair. I was stunned. It was as if someone punched me in the gut and knocked the wind out of me. 13 weeks? There was no way to confirm that it would last this long for sure. It was something we just had to wait and see. *Thir-teen weeks?*

"An episode, whether mania, depression, or mixed state, can last a couple of weeks…" I stopped listening to him. I knew what he was saying because I read about it. Basically, I had to go through all the episodes to complete a cycle. Plus, the paranoia and hallucinations had to subside, of course. I've encountered my mixed state episodes and they are no fun. At this extreme side of the spectrum, I know I will be in for a doozy. The name implies everything. During a mixed state, I don't know if I'm depressed or if I'm manic. They move so fast during this time it just looks as though I'm having really bad mood swings. One day, life sucks and I want to stay in bed all day, the next, everything is awesome and I want to go out and party all night. There is no balance.

"How do we know I haven't 'cycled' already and that this is the end?"

"We *don't* know, that's why we have to observe you."

I was still twirling my hair and noticed the movements of my wrist and fingers had increased in speed, so I stopped. I lowered my hand and crossed my arms as if trying to hug myself. This was all too sudden. But isn't that how it is? At first you are absolutely fine, then, suddenly, you have a mental breakdown out of nowhere, then you're fine again…?

"The thing with bipolar disorder—and now with psychosis—is that you never know when it will strike. You have to stay on a regimented treatment plan to ensure the symptoms will keep at bay," the Doctor started speaking again. I don't know if he was speaking the entire time, but I sat there not saying a word until something he said stuck out to me. I let out a sigh and he paused. "What is it?"

I shrugged. I finally had nothing to say. My brain felt empty at this point and all I could do was watch him move his hands from his pants pockets to mid-air in order to provide emphasis to his words.

"Are you afraid?" he asked.

I blinked slowly before answering. "Afraid? I'm terrified. I'm beyond afraid right now. Look at me. I'm stuck in a mental hospital when I could be out enjoying life," I gestured towards the window. "I'm 27 years old and I'm crazy. I just want to go back to normal and living my life. I don't know what lesson I'm supposed to learn here, but I know that I can't take advantage of my time. I get it." I let it all come out, including the tears I was holding back. I broke down. I covered my face with my hands and sobbed. Dr. Ricardi didn't move from his place beside the window. He just let me cry. "I want to go home!" I let the words come out as loud as I could muster in between my sniffles. So much for feeling emotionless. I was angry and fed up with the situation. Embarrassed by my outburst, I asked again, "how can I go home?"

Dr. Ricardi was silent.

I sat there, recovering from my emotions, also silent. It felt like hours had passed before I regained to courage to speak. "Can I ask you something?"

"Certainly." Dr. Ricardi turned and strutted towards his desk and sat down facing me.

"What medications am I on now?" my thumb returned to my mouth and I bit down. I held my breath awaiting his answer.

"I have you on a combination of lithium and quetiapine. Lithium is a mood stabilizer and quetiapine is an antipsychotic," the Doctor informed me.

"Like the Abilify?" I inquired.

"Yes."

"Why not give me that then?"

"The Abilify can cause you to get manic. Which we assume happened here. The Seroquel has a sedating effect for the first few days of treatment and I figured this would be necessary to calm your system down a bit and take a handle on you mania."

I couldn't say anything. *Could it have been that the medication that was making me better was actually putting me in jeopardy?* That's what I heard come out of Dr. Ricardi's mouth. I couldn't take what he was saying. I understood what he explained, but emotionally, I couldn't handle it.

"I'm tired," I said interrupting him. While I really was starting to get sleepy, I wanted the conversation to be over. Everything made too much sense and that was not comforting to me. I rose from my seat and headed for the door. Dr. Ricardi stood up as well and walked with me to my room.

He told me goodbye and turned to leave. As he began walking back towards the elevators, the Doctor looked over his shoulder and called out, "until tomorrow, Andrea."

Chapter 8

If you don't keep track of your moods, bipolar disorder can really hold you hostage. If you don't stay on your medication, bipolar disorder can turn you into someone you don't recognize. If you don't regularly see a therapist, bipolar disorder will make you hold everything inside until you explode. I had to learn how to manage and track my bipolar disorder so I could do everything I could in order to keep it under control. Staying on my meds was something I needed to discipline myself on. Before, I would always forget to take them, so now I have an alarm set on my phone to remind me every day. I have to see my psychologist during our scheduled appointments. I needed to make sure to keep a diary of my moods and how I felt each day to visually see any pattern I was in and to determine if I should contact either of my doctors.

I was determined to make this work. I will live with this illness for the rest of my life so I have to make treating it a regular routine like something as common sense as showering or brushing my teeth. For me, I knew a big thing was tracking my moods. I don't pay attention to the buildup, that at the end, I flip out and have no idea how I ended up there. That's what was happening. It feels like it all comes out of nowhere when the truth is, I didn't pay attention. To me, everything is so minor and I figure I'll get over it that I don't realize how the "little" emotions affect me. I end up holding so much inside, like me not wanting to be a burden on others, that when the emotions reach a max, I blow up. I just get overwhelmed because I didn't handle the emotions before it reached "blow up" status.

I took the pill bottle in my hands and closed my eyes. It was day 3 out of the hospital and I felt as if it had been months. I twisted the cap off and poured one of the white pills in my hand. I looked at it. There were no thoughts in my head. This was just something I had to do. I had to take this pill and move forward with my life. I took it and sighed. *Another day towards the rest of my life.* I wasn't sad nor disappointed. I took it in stride and realized, yes, I am crazy, and that's okay. I chuckled and picked up my laptop.

"What's so funny?" Shannon asked me as I walked out of my bedroom. She was sitting on the couch putting together her schedule for the coming week. She had been nothing less than supportive when I was discharged. While being locked in a hospital for a little over a month, she came to see me at every chance she could. Some days were better than others, but I was grateful to have a familiar face to look forward to. Now that I was out, she was still supportive. She encouraged me and tried to instill in me that I am not my disease. Yes, I have it and am living with it, but it doesn't make me a bad person… It doesn't make me less of a person.

"Just thinking about the fact that I really am a crazy person now," I chuckled again.

"You are not crazy, Drea. You simply had a breakdown. Nothing more, nothing less. Stop trying to define it and put a label on yourself."

"It was a joke. I have to find a way to look at this and find some positive humor in it all," I tried to defend myself.

She didn't retreat. "That's fine. Just don't let it become a habit, because then it will be a defense mechanism and we won't know what it is you're hiding. We don't want this to happen again."

Shannon was blunt, but she was right. We don't want this to happen again. I sat on the opposite couch facing her with my computer open. She was so into what she was writing in her notebook that during her speech she didn't look up at me once. In that moment, I envied her; her focus and determination to complete whatever she was doing. I wanted that for myself.

While I was in the hospital, I had received an email stating that an admissions decision had been made regarding my University of Cincinnati application for the mental health counseling program. I read the message a few days prior, but never logged on to the admissions website see what the decision actually was. I was nervous. I hadn't wanted something this badly since I wanted to apply to medical school. This meant that I wanted this more than I wanted to breathe at that moment. A link in an email now determined my future... At least the next two years of my life.

I typed "gmail.com" into the browser, pressed enter, and my inbox opened. I scrolled down the list of incoming mail and hovered over the one from the University's Graduate Admissions with my mouse. I inhaled deeply and held my breath. My body went numb. The subject line read, "A decision has been made on your application to UC." I clicked to open it. There was a link and a list of instructions for what to do if admitted to the University. I let my breath out slowly. I clicked the link and logged into the system. The page refreshed to show my submitted application with another link that read, "summary". Again, I took a breath and held it. I closed my eyes and clicked the link. Without opening my eyes, I let all the air out of my body. I opened my eyes and squinted at the screen, afraid of what I may see…

Admitted.

I opened my eyes fully to find myself staring at the word. I couldn't believe it. With the luck I had been having, I was sure I wasn't going to get in.

"Oh my God."

"What?" Shannon looked up from her paperwork.

"Umm… I got in."

"Got in where?"

"UC." I couldn't muster up complete sentences. I was completely surprised. Admitted.

"Oh my God! That is amazing!" Shannon squealed and jumped out of her seat. While I was awestruck, she was joyously trying to get me up and celebrating with her. She plopped down beside me and gave me a hug. "This is exciting. Congratulations!"

"Thanks," I said so passively that she was concerned.

"Isn't this what you wanted? Are you okay?"

"Yes. I'm excited, just surprised. I didn't think I would get in," I confessed.

"Why wouldn't you get in? You're smart and you know what you want. You have your own personal experience with mental health… Why wouldn't they choose you over somebody else?" She looked me in my face and continued, "this is what I'm talking about. You have to become confident in yourself and your abilities to be great. If you can't do that, you won't succeed. Then, you'll be walking around here, like, 'oh, I knew I wouldn't be able to do so-and-so. I knew I would fail.' And that's not fair to yourself."

I knew she was one-hundred percent right. I had to get in the mindset that I am, indeed, good enough to have what I want. If I don't, I'll always be a victim to any situation I'm in. I had to celebrate this incredible win!

"Let's go get some drinks!" It was noon on a Wednesday and I wanted to celebrate with vodka. For whatever reason, I liked the way alcohol made me feel and I was ready to indulge.

"I have to go back to work," Shannon laughed. "But maybe tonight when I get off."

I giggled with her. It was a pretty forward request for the middle of the day. I agreed and hugged her back. She returned to her spot with her planner and continued writing. I turned my attention to my phone as I sat my laptop aside and crossed my legs Indian style on the couch. I began to text James the good news.

'Guess what?' I typed and waited for a response. Almost immediately, he typed back.

'What?'

'I got into UC!' I replied with a few smiley face emojis to support how elated I was. *'I wasn't sure if I would get in.'*

'Why wouldn't you get in?' He questioned, echoing Shannon's words from a few moments earlier. Why didn't I believe in my ability to get accepted into a school I once attended, interviewed well at, and showed a genuine interest in their program? It only made sense for me to be accepted.

I don't know, I thought. I didn't respond to

James's message, but I did let him know I was excited. *'We're going to celebrate tonight with drinks and food!!'* I couldn't wait. This would be my first time venturing out of the house since I left the hospital. I was ready to see what the world offered after psychosis. Would everything look fresh and new? Would colors be vibrant and bright, now? I didn't know, but I looked forward to it.

'You should write a book,' he suggested.

'Why would I write a book? To relive a miserable time in my life? No thank you.' Having gone through what I went through in the hospital, I knew that mental health was something I wanted to pursue, for sure. I felt as though having the personal experience to understand my clients and what they were going through was a necessary component in order to be able to connect with them. I would have the knowledge to not only understand their issue from a world of theory, but also from a personal standpoint, and that was important to me. Now I was even more motivated to get started at University of Cincinnati.

He didn't reply. I changed the subject. *'How have you been? You missed me bothering you all the time?'* I teased.

'*Actually, I did. I've just been working. Nothing's been different here.*'

'*Sounds like fun,*' I typed sarcastically. I gripped my cup and sipped the iced water within it. I was gone for what felt like ages, how could things still be the same? Or at least, how could nothing spectacular have happened while I was away? *Was he holding back information to make me not feel bad for missing out?* I looked at my phone. It was okay if James was lying. If something amazing happened I really wouldn't want to know about it. Knowing would only bring me down because I wasn't here to experience it myself.

James didn't say anything after that. From our prior conversations, I knew he was working hard and was sick. So he was either sleeping or working. I didn't take offense. I took the halt in our conversation to mean an opportunity to text other people who warranted a "must know" label from me. At that time, I sent messages to my other best friends and let them know what decision had been made. Everyone was congratulatory and wished me the best. I stopped saying that I was surprised and just accepted each of the celebrations by text with a sincere thank you. It was hard to step outside of myself and remain so positive. After so long of being the Negative Nancy and the What-If Wendy, it was a welcomed change to finally be Positive Drea; even if it was for a small moment during the larger scheme of things.

I let out a sigh and uncrossed my legs. I sat my computer in my lap and turned it on. By now, it had shut down and needed rebooting. Once everything had loaded, I went to the acceptance letter and read it. *I really got in.* I needed to accept my acceptance and confirm my enrollment. At least that's what the letter said to do. I clicked back to the first screen and highlighted the enroll button. In that moment I was so happy. I dramatically raised my arm and dropped it down to click on the button. It was done. I officially enrolled and was on my way to becoming a University of Cincinnati student once more.

Wait. This was strange.

There was no anxiety, no worry, nothing but positive energy. "What is this?" I queried to myself out loud.

"What's what?" Shannon asked not looking up from her schedule planning. She was so quiet and engulfed in her work that I forgot she was there with me.

"Nothing. Just thinking out loud. Sorry."

"Hm," she uttered in place of a real word.

Here I go again, trying to find the negative in something so good. I picked up my computer and walked back to my bedroom. I should still feel excited about getting into the school of my dreams for a second time, but I was preoccupied by why I wasn't feeling a certain way. That, in and of itself, was making me anxious. I closed the door behind me, placed the computer on my desk, and sat on the bed. I was waiting for my heart to beat out of my chest and my hands to start sweating. None of that happened. I felt normal. A recognizable, absolutely normal sensation rode a wave through my body. There was no irrational response to something minor. Yes, in that moment anxiety took over, but it wasn't anything I couldn't manage. I took a breath and laid back. It finally felt good to feel normal. I smiled.

I pulled out my computer and opened Microsoft Word. I began typing. **The Bipolar Black Girl** flowed from my fingers and I stopped. I stared at the words. *Was I really going to share my story, again? Was I going to relive my epic time in the hospital just to prove that black people suffer from mental illnesses, too?* I had no idea how I was going to write it nor what I was going to write so I just sat there looking at the four words I had on the screen. **<u>The Bipolar Black Girl.</u>** I knew I wanted it to be different than my last book in that it would be intentional and read like a story, but I didn't know where to begin. I took my hands from the keyboard and looked about the room. Where would be a good starting point?

Start at the hospital and you can edit it from there. Just start writing.

I started typing. The words appeared on the screen effortlessly. Within a few days I was already at 24 thousand words with more to go. This was therapeutic. I didn't have a psychologist or therapist yet, so being able to get myself out of my own head though writing really helped me cope. Before I knew it, I was done. There was nothing more to the story. I let out a sigh. This meant I had to find something else to keep me occupied before school started. Nonetheless, the book was finished and I had something else to be proud of.

11:23 am the clock on my phone read. I had awakened and started editing the book right away that I hadn't realized how much time had passed. I missed my 9am appointment with my pills. I sat my laptop aside, got out of my bed, and grabbed the two prescription bottles off my desk. I opened one and poured a round, white pill into my hand and closed the bottle. I put the pill down and looked at it. I was feeling normal and the thought popped into my head. A thought I didn't think of in weeks. *Do I really need this?* It was an intrusive thought that meant nothing. I quickly countered with, *I absolutely need it. That's why I have it.* It's more than just feeling well today, it's about feeling well for the rest of my life. I unscrewed the second bottle and let the pink pill fall into my palm. It was like second nature by now. I picked up both the pills and let them into my mouth. I drank from the water bottle near my bed and guzzled down the medication. It was done and now I could move on with my day. I grabbed my phone and opened the Facebook app. I typed in the status bar: *#AdventuresWithDrea* and snapped a quick picture of my computer screen.

There was nothing, then, there was everything. Not a single thing was holding me back and it was a great feeling. Today, like every other day to come, was the first day of the rest of my life and I embraced it.

Andrea Elizabeth Paul

Epilogue

There was nothing, then, there was everything. The feeling that rose in my body was overwhelming. My body tensed and my breathing shallowed. My face flushed and my palms began to sweat. I stared out the window of my car and looked up at the building that stood before me. I let out a huge breath and forced my body to relax. A driver beeped their car horn at me. I stopped in the middle of the road to look at my future. "Teacher's College" the sign read. I took it in. Today would be the first day (or night) of classes and I was excited and nervous. I drove a few feet in front of me and parked my car on the busy street behind a silver Honda Civic. My new Mazda3 fit perfectly in the small space. While I pushed my credit card into the parking meter, I sighed. I couldn't hold back the anxiety I had. I was happy to be here and knew I made the right decision. There wasn't an ounce of regret or remorse in my mind. I was enthusiastic to continue learning about myself and others like me. Counseling made sense and I was ready to finally pursue a passion of mine and become a professional.

The Bipolar Black Girl was written as a small glimpse into the mind of someone, a minority woman, at that, suffering daily from the illness. I wanted to get people—you—to understand that it is possible to be a survivor of this disorder and be a black woman. I wanted to dispel the myths of the idea of what society and the African-American community defines as "crazy." By anyone's standards and observations of me (and I asked, strangers and friends alike), I, Andrea Elizabeth Paul, seem like I "am very well put together," "a go getter," "smart," "easy-going," and "composed." If they only understood that I was diagnosed with Bipolar I disorder, they would immediately look at me confused. After telling a stranger this news, I was met with a confused glance and tilt of the head as if to non-verbally ask me "really?" This will be followed by a quick fixing of their face to show some type of unnecessary empathy and a statement like, "I never would have guessed."

Mental illness is more complex than someone talking to themselves or seeing things. Mental illness includes having a sense of confidence you wouldn't normally have, not believing in your own abilities, feeling down for no reason at all, being unreasonably optimistic, being tense around other people, losing touch with reality… Of course these are all oversimplifications in the grander scheme of mental health, but they all carry some weight when it comes to a mental health diagnosis of some sort.

Bipolar disorder, depression, anxiety, borderline personality disorder, schizophrenia, eating disorders, substance abuse, ADD, ADHD, cyclothymia, narcisstic personality disorder, obsessive compulsive disorder, or any other disorder or illness deserves recognition and awareness in the black community. These run in families for generations without being addressed due to the stigma surrounding mental illness, the untruth that "everything is fine," or the feeling that the person is alone in feeling like they do. Guess what? These are all lies we tell ourselves in order to be perceived as strong by others. But why do we do this to ourselves, black women, especially? Why do we choose to suffer through the pain our respective diseases puts us through? For one, I believe it is because of the lack of knowledge surrounding mental health, in general. We are quick to claim we are sick and go see a doctor for a physical ailment, but hide when we have a mental symptom because we simply do not know what to do.

In light, it is okay to be "sick in the head" as long as you acknowledge that something is wrong and seek help for it. It is absolutely acceptable to schedule an appointment with a mental health care provider if you feel unwell. Realize that you are not alone and that there is a whole community of people rooting for you to rise above your illness. Remember, you are not your bipolar/ depression/ anxiety/ etc. and it doesn't make you a bad person for having it. Just be sure to get the help you need when you need it. Know that it's okay to not always be okay.

For those of you not suffering with a mental disorder, support those you know. Learn what you can about mental health, one, to keep yourself healthy, and two, to be prepared if someone you know confides in you about their mental status. The more you know, the more you can help someone in need. You can be an advocate for those who cannot, or will not, advocate for themselves. Be the voice of positivity and uplifting others may need.

Again, I wrote this book to bring attention to mental illness and the fact that it is prevalent in the African-American community. By bringing awareness to disorders like my own, you won't discount that the girl you sit next to on the bus or the guy you work with lives with a mental disorder. You may stop saying "you don't look crazy/ you don't seem mental/ you can't be" to anyone who confides in you. In the beginning, it's hard enough to accept that you had a disorder that impairs how you view "reality", it's even harder to have people look at you "like you're crazy" for actually living with a mental disorder. Don't be that person. Be sensitive and realize mental disorders don't look the same on everyone. I'm bipolar, yet I am one of the most patient, calmest people you may ever meet. On the other hand, someone in the hospital with me while I was in Atlanta was so aggressive and loud. But we have the same diagnosis. Don't judge us. Don't tell me "well, you're not like them…" News flash. I am just like them. We are living every single day with something we can't control. Yes, we can manage it with medication and appropriate therapy, but we cannot control when our disorder will pull us in one direction or another. Please understand this. Be the solution to helping make the stigma and negativity surrounding mental illness a distant memory. Let's start the conversation about bringing awareness to mental health by changing how we talk and think about it and by promoting proper education around mental disorders and their treatment.

Signed,

The Bipolar Black Girl

Andrea Elizabeth Paul

Andrea Elizabeth Paul

CPSIA information can be obtained at www.ICGtesting.com
Printed in the USA
LVOW10s1507240616

494011LV00012B/268/P